INTERME   ISTORY

FREE AT LAST?
RACE RELATIONS IN THE USA
1918–1968

JOHN A. KERR

HODDER
GIBSON
AN HACHETTE UK COMPANY

PREFACE

History has no beginning but books have and writers must choose a point of departure. In the case of *Free at Last?*, the departure time, announced by the Scottish Qualifications Authority, is 1918 and the arrival time is 1968. There is a good rationale for that and course content must rest easily with other unit topics. However, in selecting 1918 as a starting point, one risks giving the impression that Civil Rights is a twentieth century phenomenon and that history can be packaged. Issues which are timeless are presented in a pre-formed way so that students can study, complete instruments of assessments, answer a combination of internal and external assessments and then forget.

The criterion for most students therefore is not 'need to know' but is 'need to know in order to pass exam.' Once the latter is completed, the former is redundant.

In this book I have deliberately gone into some detail about the years before 1918 and, more importantly, raised issues by merely touching on developments after 1968. I would urge all educators to take time out of a packed syllabus to set the issue of US Civil Rights in its historical context and at the end to draw attention to the punctuation in the title of the course – Free at Last, question mark.

History is not dead. There is always an unanswered question to provoke further thought.

John A. Kerr 2000

ACKNOWLEDGEMENTS

The publishers would like to thank the following for permission to reproduce photographs in this book:

Associated Press (53 bottom left, 75, 100 top left, 109, 113, 114 both, 117); Brown Brothers (11, 12 top, 32 bottom); Camera Press Ltd (57, 100 bottom left); Corbis (6 both, 13 right, 20, 23 bottom, 27, 37, 38 both, 42 both, 46, 47, 53 top left, 56, 66, 70, 76, 79 both, 84, 85, 86, 91, 100 right, 106); Culver Pictures Inc., New York (12 bottom, 14); Franklin Roosevelt Library, New York (32 top); Hulton Getty (9 right, 41, 60, 94); Los Angeles County Museum of Art, Los Angeles County Fund (13 left); Mansell/Time Inc. (9 left); Marshall Cavendish (26, 53 right); Popperfoto (23 top, 108); Robert N. Hower (25)

The publishers would also like to thank the following for permission to reproduce material in this book:

Penguin for the extract from *The Eyes on the Prize Civil Rights Reader*

Every effort has been made to trace and acknowledge ownership of copyright. The publishers will be glad to make suitable arrangements with any copyright holders whom it has not been possible to contact.

DEDICATION

To my Mum and Dad, thanks

Orders: please contact Bookpoint Ltd, 130 Milton Park, Abingdon, Oxon OX14 4SB. Telephone: (44) 01235 827720, Fax: (44) 01235 400454. Lines are open from 9.00–5.00, Monday to Saturday, with a 24 hour message answering service. You can also order through our website www.hoddereducation.co.uk

A catalogue record for this title is available from The British Library

ISBN-13: 978-0-340-78009-1

Published by Hodder Gibson, 2a Christie Street, Paisley, PA1 1NB. Tel: 0141 8481609; Fax: 0141 8896315; e-mail: hoddergibson@hodder.co.uk

First published 2000
Impression number   15   14
Year   2013

Copyright © 2000 John Kerr

Headline's policy is to use papers that are natural, renewable and recyclable products and made from wood grown in sustainable forests. The logging and manufacturing processes are expected to conform to the environmental regulations of the country of origin.

Cover photo from Associated Press
Illustrated by Richard Duszczak and Hardlines.
Typeset by Fakenham Prepress Solutions, Fakenham, Norfolk
Printed in Great Britain for Hodder Gibson 2a Christie Street, Paisley, PA1 1NB, Scotland, UK by CPI Group (UK) Ltd, Croydon, CR0 4YY.

CONTENTS

Before 1900

1861	American Civil War began
1863	Slavery abolished in USA
1865	American Civil War ended
1870	Black American adult males get right to vote
1886	Statue of Liberty completed
1896	Supreme Court decision allows 'Separate but Equal' segregation

1900s

1907	Dillingham Commission
1909	NAACP founded

1910s

1915	Ku Klux Klan was re-established
1917	USA joined World War One
1917	Chicago race riots
1918	End of World War One

1920s

1920	Sacco and Vanzetti arrested for robbery and murder
1921	Immigration Act limited immigration
1921	Tulsa race riot
1924	Another Immigration Act cut immigration further
1927	Sacco and Vanzetti were executed
1929	Martin Luther King was born

1930s

1930	The Nation of Islam was founded
1931	Scottsboro boys were arrested and sentenced to death

1940s

1941	A. Philip Randolph planned March on Washington
1941	USA joined World War Two
1942	CORE founded

1950s

1953	Martin Luther King married Coretta Scott
1954	Brown v the Topeka Board of Education

1954	Supreme Court said 'Separate but Equal' must stop
1955	Montgomery bus boycott started
1955	Emmett Till murdered
1957	First Black students tried to join Central High School, Little Rock
1957	Southern Christian Leadership Conference (SCLC) founded
1957	Civil Rights Act passed

1960s

1960	Martin Luther King president of SCLC
1960	First sit-in at Greensboro, North Carolina
1960	Students Non-violent Coordinating Committee founded
1963	Martin Luther King made 'I Have a Dream' speech
1963	Protests in Birmingham, Alabama
1963	March on Washington
1963	Sixteenth Street Church Bombing, Alabama
1963	John F. Kennedy assassinated
1963	Malcolm X split with the Nation of Islam
1964	Martin Luther King awarded Nobel Peace Prize
1964	Civil Rights Act
1965	Watts ghetto riots
1965	Selma to Montgomery march
1965	Voting Rights Act
1965	Malcolm X was murdered
1966	The Black Panther Party founded
1966	Martin Luther King and the SCLC made the Chicago Plan
1966	Stokely Carmichael became leader of SNCC
1968	Civil Rights Act
1968	Kerner Commission set up
1968	Martin Luther King shot dead
1968	Mexico Olympic Games

1980s

| 1988 | Jesse Jackson failed to be chosen as Presidential candidate |

1990s

| 1998 | James Byrd, a Black American, killed by white racists linked to the Ku Klux Klan |

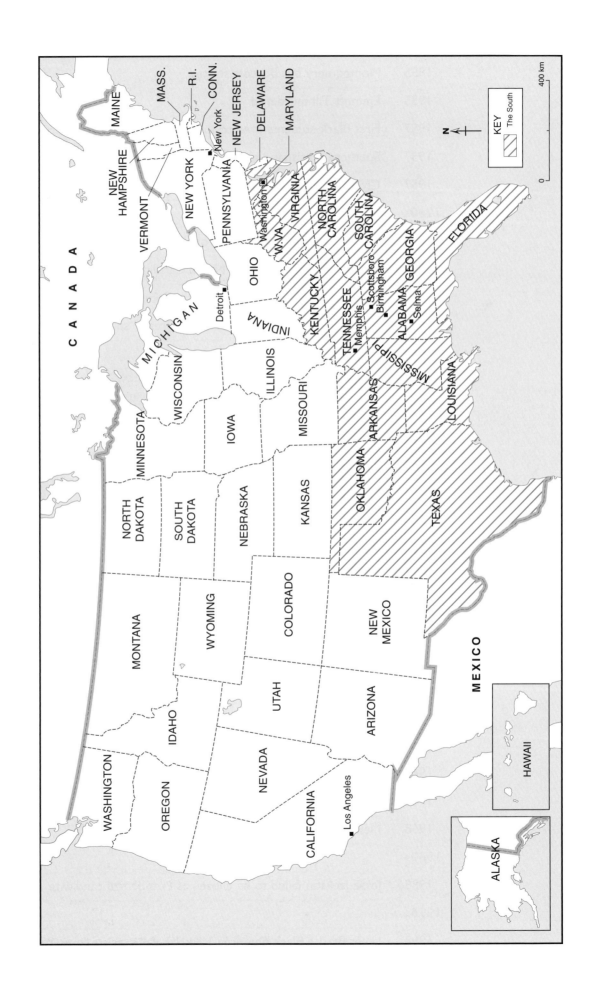

INTRODUCTION

The United States of America is sometimes called the land of the free and the land of opportunity. Today most of the USA's population, apart from Native Americans, are descended from people who migrated to the USA in search of a better life.

In 1776 the USA declared itself to be a free and independent country. Until then it had been ruled by the British. The leaders of the USA wrote a Declaration of Independence that made it clear why they wanted to be free.

All men are created equal, they are endowed by their Creator with certain unalienable Rights, among these are Life and Liberty, and the pursuit of Happiness.

This is what it means...

Everyone in America has the right to get on with their life as they want. Nobody has the right to stop American people from being as happy and successful as they can be.

George Washington, the first US President.

In the early years of the twentieth century the USA was growing fast. Immigrants from Europe flooded into the USA. Many of them found happiness and success. But many Americans were not happy. They were Black Americans who found that the USA was not a land of opportunity.

Although this book ends in 1968 an event from the 1980s might help you question whether the USA has become a land of opportunity for all.

In the 1980s a political party in America was choosing a person to stand for election as US President. They chose Michael Dukakis, a man whose parents had been immigrants from Greece.

In the space of one generation Michael Dukakis had moved from being the son of an immigrant to being a top politician in the USA. For the Dukakis family the USA was the land of opportunity.

Michael Dukakis had to choose someone to be his 'second in

Michael Dukakis

Jesse Jackson

command'. It seemed likely that he would choose a man called Jesse Jackson who was almost as popular as Dukakis. Jackson's family had been in the USA for a long time. However Jackson was not chosen.

Many people think Jackson was not chosen because his skin is Black. Perhaps it was too risky to select a Black American for an important political job in the USA. Perhaps people would not vote for him because of racial prejudice. For Jesse Jackson, America was not the same free land of opportunity that it was for Michael Dukakis.

Most of this book is about the struggle of Black Americans to win Civil Rights or, in other words, the same rights to find happiness and success that had been promised to all Americans almost 200 years earlier. At the end of the book you'll be asked to think if the USA became the land of freedom.

This course has a subtitle which is *Free at Last?* – don't forget the question mark.

THE AMERICAN DREAM

'*An American is somebody who came from somewhere else to become someone else*'.

In 1900 the USA was a mixture of all sorts of people. Some of them had recently arrived from Europe or Asia. Others were the children or grandchildren of earlier immigrants.

In 1915 the USA was described as follows: '*America is like a huge Melting Pot. We will mix the races together to create a new person – an American.*'

SOURCE 1.1 *America was likened to a huge melting pot*

During the later 1800s living and working conditions had worsened for millions of Europeans. At the same time the United States entered a period of incredible prosperity. After the 1880s, the USA needed more and more unskilled workers to fill the growing number of factory jobs. At the same time southern and eastern Europeans, were attracted to the growing industries in the United States. Demand attracted its own supply. Millions of Europeans, unable to bear the pressures of unemployment, depressions and famines began to see America as a land of opportunity. Unfortunately, their dreams of wealth and free land seldom became reality.

At first most *immigrants* to the USA came from Northern Europe, especially Britain, Ireland, Germany and Scandinavia. By 1900 a new wave of immigrants were heading to the USA from poorer areas of Europe such as Poland, Italy and Russia. These people moved for the same reasons as everyone else did. They can be split into push and pull reasons:

- a *push* reason is anything that makes people want to escape their difficulties
- a *pull* reason is anything that attracts people and makes them want to move

The promise of work, enough food to eat and political freedom were more than enough to attract people to emigrate to the United States. Immigrants from abroad fled to the United States seeking opportunities promised to them by relatives, friends, agents and a growing economy. The USA was like a magnet of hope and the Statue of Liberty was the light which promised a bright future. Improvements in steamship technology also had an effect on migration – journeys to America became faster and safer.

SOURCE 1.2 *Families like this were happy to reach America*

SOURCE 1.3 *The Statue of Liberty was a symbol of new hope for immigrants*

The Statue of Liberty was usually the first thing immigrants saw as they approached the USA. The Statue was built in 1886 in New York harbour.

When they saw the Statue of Liberty many immigrants often broke down in tears of joy. Immigrants such as Jews, who were escaping persecution, were happy at the thought of a free, democratic society. Immigrants escaping hunger and poverty wept with happiness at the thought of riches and an easy life. The Statue holds a torch of freedom and the words at the bottom of the Statue sum up the reason why many people chose to *migrate* to the USA.

SOURCE 1.4

'Give me your tired, your poor,
Your huddled masses yearning to breathe free,
The wretched refuse of your teeming shore.
Send these the homeless, tempest tossed to me
I lift my lamp beside the golden door.'

Chapter Summary
- Most people in the USA today are descended from immigrants.
- Immigrants came to the USA looking for a fresh start and a better life.
- At first it was hoped that immigrants would leave their old lives behind and mix together as Americans. That was called the Melting Pot idea of America.

QUESTION PRACTICE

Source A is taken from an interview with Joe Swerling, a Polish Jew, newly arrived in New York in 1900.

SOURCE A

I decided to take my family to America so I could live and work in peace and safety.

1 How useful is this source as evidence of reasons why people emigrated to the USA? *Outcome 3*

2 Explain the difference between a push reason and a pull reason for emigration. *Outcome 2*

QUESTION PRACTICE

Source B is adapted from an interview with Colette McInstry, an Irish immigrant to the USA in 1900.

SOURCE B

America was like a dream where we could all become rich. I would find a job, find a husband and start a new life.

3 Compare sources A and B. In what ways and for what reasons do sources A and B differ from one another? *Outcome 3*

2
IMMIGRANTS IN A NEW LAND – THE IMMIGRANT EXPERIENCE

In this chapter you will find out:
- about the experiences of new immigrants arriving in America
- what is meant by 'The American Dream'
- why slum housing increased in US cities
- how and why politicians helped new immigrants
- what the letters WASP mean.

ELLIS ISLAND – 'THE ISLE OF TEARS'

From 1892 immigrants were taken to Ellis Island in New York harbour before they were allowed to enter the USA. Immigrants had to wait on board their ship until they were 'processed'.

SOURCE 2.1 *Immigrants had to wait on deck before being taken ashore to be 'processed'*

All immigrants had been given numbers and when they landed on Ellis Island they were taken in groups of about thirty to be 'processed'. First of all they were checked by a doctor who had in his hand a piece of chalk. After a quick inspection of an immigrant the doctor might chalk an *H* on his or her back which meant suspected heart disease or an *F* for any rashes or blotches on their face. There was one mark that every family feared. It was a circle with a cross in the middle of it. The sign meant 'feeble minded' and it meant the family would be sent back to where they had just come from. For them, Ellis Island was an 'island of tears'.

SOURCE 2.2 *Immigrants were checked for infectious diseases*

Once the medical inspection was passed, immigrants had a series of questions to answer such as 'do you have a job waiting for you?'. If the inspections were all passed the immigrant was given a landing card. With a landing card the immigrant became a new American. He or she would catch the ferry to New York and start the search for the *American Dream* .

WHAT IS THE AMERICAN DREAM?

The American Dream is the belief that anyone can be a success. Immigrants travelled to America in the hope that they would find a better standard of living, get a better job and give a better start in life to their children. The American Dream was really hope – hope that no matter what your background was, you could make a fresh start in America and if you worked hard then you would be successful.

However before they found the American Dream, new immigrants to the USA faced a series of problems. These problems are summarised in Source 2.3.

SOURCE 2.3 *Immigrants had to deal with many problems as they climbed towards the American Dream*

CITY SLUMS

The great majority of immigrants settled in cities. Immigrant populations were highest in four of America's largest cities at the time (New York, Boston, Pittsburgh, and Chicago).

Slum housing was a very serious problem faced by immigrants to the USA. Slum tenements were often five or six stories high and honeycombed with tiny rooms which lacked light and proper sanitation. These slums became centres of disease and crime but they were also the first rung on the ladder for many immigrants who came to America searching for a better life.

The photograph in Source 2.5 shows a family who look proud and pleased that they have started a new life in America.

SOURCE 2.4 *As more and more people crowded into cities, slum housing became a serious problem*

SOURCE 2.5 *This family are clearly proud of their new home*

SOURCE 2.6 *Most immigrants crowded into the cities*

The slums that many new immigrants crowded into got even worse as more immigrants arrived looking for cheap housing. New York had the worst examples of overcrowded and poor slum conditions, partly because it was the city that most immigrants poured into when they first arrived in the USA. However New York was not the only city with slums. Slums existed wherever recent immigrants crowded together.

Immigrants had always tended to live with people from similar backgrounds, culture and language. By the early 1900s the thousands of immigrants from Southern and Eastern Europe felt alone and far from home. They added to the pattern of immigrant housing that was growing in many American cities. In these cities separate communities became identified by names such as Little Germany or Irishtown. If you had visited an American city in the early 1900s it would have seemed as if the crowds in the streets were proof that there really was a melting pot. People from all sorts of backgrounds with different cultures and languages were mixing together. However if you listened carefully you could have told whether you were in 'Little Italy' or 'Little Russia'. As late as the 1950s the son of an immigrant described Chicago like this:

SOURCE 2.7

To the north was Germany, to the west was Poland and to the south was Ireland.

The idea that American cities were like giant jigsaws of different nationalities of people is supported by another young immigrant who said:

SOURCE 2.8

Growing up in a melting pot's tenement district (of New York) in the heat of the migration to America, young Leo avoided trouble by adopting an Irish or German or Italian or whatever accent was necessary to keep out of trouble.

WHAT DO YOU THINK?

Why would immigrants, newly arrived in the USA, choose to live in slum areas?

IMMIGRANTS AND POLITICS

Most immigrants had no idea about voting or having a say in the way the country was run. America was called the land of the free but many immigrants had no clear idea of what political freedom meant. Nor did they know much about how the political system worked. The result of such lack of knowledge was that many immigrants became the followers of any politician who offered them help. Bribery was sometimes used but mostly immigrants were happy to vote for any politician who looked after the needs of their family.

SOURCE 2.9

In exchange for your vote … he would … get you a job, he would get your son out of trouble, he would hound the landlord to repair your stove or bathtub. In bad times he brought up coal and food. He knew when the baby was coming and would get a doctor.

But it would be very wrong to think that immigrants were stupid and did what they were told. Immigrants had shown by their willingness to move that they had 'get up and go'. Immigrant families learned fast and many immigrant families continued to support certain politicians mainly because these politicians kept in touch with what the new Americans wanted.

Immigrants also became politically powerful. As early as the 1880s Irish immigrants began to dominate the political systems in many large cities and later on in this book you will find out about a US president called John F. Kennedy. He was a descendant of Irish Catholics who had emigrated to America in the nineteenth century.

In New York City, an organisation called Tammany Hall influenced city politics. It attracted a lot of support from immigrant Irish people by helping immigrants find jobs and become US citizens and by assisting the poor.

Source 2.10 shows how any ambitious man had to bow and scrape to the Irish controlled city government which is shown by a large Irishman with Irish flags hanging from his chair.

SOURCE 2.10 *In some cities Irish politicians controlled what went on*

PUCK.

THEY ALL DO IT—CRINGING BEFORE THE IRISH VOTE AND SUPPORT.

However real power was still in the hands of *WASP* politicians and they tried very hard to keep it that way.

WASPS AND THE NEW IMMIGRANTS

Families who had been in the USA for a long time and were descended from early settlers, especially from Britain, thought they were the most important people in the USA. They were nicknamed **WASPs**. They were **White**, they were from the **Anglo-Saxon** race of people in Northern Europe and they were mostly **Protestant**.

Look at the first letters of the bold words and what do you get? – W – A – S – P!

SOURCE 2.11 *Wasps were White Anglo-Saxon Protestants*

The Wasps did not like any challenges to their power. Wasps thought of themselves as 'old immigrants' – the people who had made America strong and powerful. The Wasp families did not like the wave of 'new' immigrants who were flooding into America from Southern and Eastern Europe and from Asia.

Wasps controlled most of America's big business and government.

If Wasps were at 'the top of the heap' in terms of power in America, at the bottom of the heap was America's Black population.

BLACK AMERICANS

Black Americans had not chosen to go to the USA. Most of America's Black population were descended from Africans who were captured and taken to the USA to be used as slaves.

For thousands of Black Americans in the early twentieth century, America was not a free and equal land of opportunity. As one Black worker in Alabama said in 1920:

SOURCE 2.12

Ain't no thing for us called the American Dream. We just see the nightmare.

Chapter summary

◆ Immigrants arrived looking for the American Dream.

◆ The American Dream was the hope that no matter how poor you were, by working hard you could become rich in America.

◆ At first, many immigrants lived in city slums.

◆ 'Wasps' meant White Anglo-Saxon Protestants.

◆ 'Wasps' were people who believed they were better than new immigrants.

◆ 'Wasps' had a lot of power in the USA.

QUESTION PRACTICE

SOURCE A is from an interview with an old immigrant.

Apartments had no heating. Running water was only available in the filthy hall. The smell was terrible and in winter we froze. But we froze back in Russia so what's the difference? At least now we had a dream to aim for.

I How does Source A help explain why so many immigrants were prepared to live in such bad conditions when they arrived in the USA? *Outcome 2*

Look at the photographs in this chapter.

2 Why are they useful sources of evidence about the experience of immigrants to the USA in the early twentieth century? *Outcome 3*

QUESTION PRACTICE

3 Why did some groups of people in America have more power than others? *Outcome 2*

SOURCE B is what a recent historian wrote about the New York slums.

Every block had it gambling dens, its prostitutes and its gangsters. Immigrant crime was a threat to the American way of life.

SOURCE C is from the memories of an old immigrant.

The streets of New York were paved with gold – at least it was as good as gold to us. There were markets groaning with food, there was no military on horseback and no whips. To a boy like me it was a giant friendship club.

4 In what ways do sources B and C differ about life in the New York slums? *Outcome 3*

3 IMMIGRATION IN THE 1920s ENOUGH – NO MORE!

In this chapter you will find out:
◆ what is meant by an 'open door policy'
◆ why America stopped its 'open door policy' for immigrants
◆ why America passed new laws to cut the numbers of immigrants
◆ the new laws discriminated against people who were not 'Wasps'

This chapter is about changing attitudes towards immigration in the 1920s.

Through most of the nineteenth century American leaders felt that immigration helped the United States economy. Businessmen were happy to see waves of immigrants arriving to provide cheap labour for the factories. However, businessmen began to change their minds as trades unions grew larger and more powerful and strikes became more common. Americans thought that immigrants from countries like Russia were the cause of strikes and riots. In the late 1890s an American businessman wrote,

SOURCE 3.1 Francis A. Walker, *The Atlantic Monthly*, June 1896

The problems which confront us to-day are serious enough without being complicated and made worse by the addition of millions of Hungarians, Italians, Poles and Russian Jews.

THE 'OPEN DOOR' STARTS TO CLOSE

For a long time America was proud of its ' *open door* ' policy. That policy meant almost anyone could enter the USA providing they were not 'feeble minded', extremely poor or had a serious disease.

However the 'open door' policy did not apply to everyone. Before 1900 the USA had cut Oriental or Asian immigration. The Chinese Exclusion Act of 1882 was the first significant law restricting immigration into the United States. In 1902 Chinese immigration was made illegal. In 1907 the Japanese government promised to stop the emigration of its citizens to the USA. Soon, however, Americans were complaining about European immigrants as well. For example, a law passed by Congress in 1921 encouraged immigration from Western European countries such as Germany, Great Britain, Ireland, and Scandinavia because the US government believed immigrants from these countries were more likely to become 'good' Americans. Meanwhile, the law discouraged immigration from Eastern and Southern Europe. By 1918 the USA's 'open door' was closing and US policy towards immigrants was becoming more racist.

THE DILLINGHAM COMMISSION

Until about 1890, the millions of immigrants who settled in the USA came mostly from Britain, Ireland, Germany, Scandinavia and from other countries in Northwestern Europe. It was not until the early twentieth century that the majority of immigrants came from countries such as Turkey, Italy or Greece in Southeastern Europe. In 1907 the US government wanted to know more about the 'problem of immigration' so it set up the Dillingham Commission.

The Dillingham Commission discovered that since the 1880s immigrants had come mainly from Southern and Eastern Europe. The Commission thought that immigrants from places like Austria-Hungary, Russia, Italy, Turkey, Lithuania, Rumania, and Greece were inferior compared to the Wasp-type immigrants who had come before 1890.

The Commission recommended that literacy tests be used to make it harder for 'inferior immigrants' to get into the USA. In other words if an immigrant could not read or write he or she would find it difficult to get into the USA. However many thousands of immigrants still got into the USA.

In 1918 the Great War ended and a new flood of immigrants from south eastern Europe prepared to cross over the Atlantic to find a new life in America. However attitudes in America towards these new immigrants were getting tougher. Americans blamed many of their problems on the new immigrants. Unemployment rose, there were lots of strikes and even letter-bomb campaigns against politicians.

The answer to America's problems seemed to be to stop immigration, especially those from 'undesirable' parts of the world. It seemed as if the words on the Statue of Liberty had lost their meaning. It was almost as if these words could have been rewritten as in Source 3.2.

Send only WASPS Immigrants we like! Don't send us problems, don't send us strife!

SOURCE 3.2

WHAT DO YOU THINK?

Is it fair to call US policy towards immigrants racist by the early 1900s?

WHY DID ATTITUDES TOWARDS IMMIGRATION CHANGE SO MUCH AFTER 1918?

◆ *Many Americans feared revolution.*
In 1917 the Russian Revolution happened. The revolution was supposed to be the first in a chain of workers' revolutions that would spread Communism throughout the world under the slogan 'Workers of the World Unite.'

Americans feared Communism might spread to the USA. Many Americans were scared that the increasing numbers of immigrants from Russia and Eastern Europe were communists who would try to take over America. This fear was called 'the red scare'. 'Red' was a nickname for a communist.

In 1919 there was a huge wave of strikes in the USA. There was a nationwide strike of steelworkers. The strikers were unskilled and semi-skilled workers, many of whom were recent immigrants from Southern and Eastern Europe. Therefore, many Americans claimed that the strikes were caused by revolutionary immigrants. They believed if nothing was done to stop the immigrants then America would face more problems.

◆ *Many Americans feared that more immigrants would make jobs and houses even harder to obtain.*
There was high unemployment in America just after the Great War. While trade unions were trying to get better working conditions for their members, employers were prepared to break strikes by employing immigrant workers to replace the strikers.

Immigrants also created more pressure on scarce housing in the poorer areas of cities. No wonder American workers saw new immigrants as a threat to their standard of living. A Trade Union leader said in 1918:

SOURCE 3.3

Anything done to improve our conditions or wages is wrecked by Italian or Polish workers who are prepared to work longer hours and for less wages.

◆ *Racism was another reason why immigration was cut.*
Many Americans were Wasps in the sense their families had come from Northern Europe. Many of these people disliked the new immigrants from Southern Europe who were poor, often illiterate and belonged to a different race from themselves. As an American called William Aspen said in 1918:

SOURCE 3.4

America must be kept pure and not turned into a second rate power by second rate people.

QUICK REVISION

Find the section in this chapter called *Why did attitudes towards immigration change so much after 1918?* Draw a spider diagram similar to the one on this page.

Use the information in that chapter and the word box to help you complete your diagram.

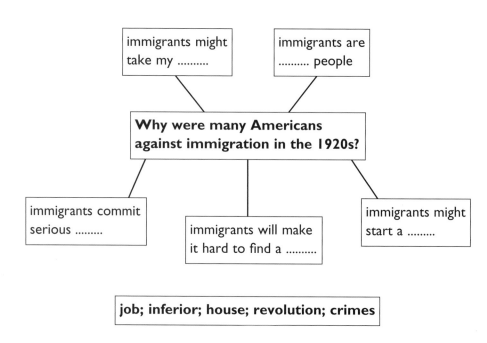

immigrants might take my ....

immigrants are .... people

Why were many Americans against immigration in the 1920s?

immigrants commit serious ....

immigrants will make it hard to find a ....

immigrants might start a ....

job; inferior; house; revolution; crimes

CASE STUDY

THE SACCO AND VANZETTI TRIAL

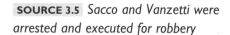
SOURCE 3.5 *Sacco and Vanzetti were arrested and executed for robbery*

Distrust of people with different ideas who came from Southeastern Europe reached its peak with the trial of Nicola Sacco and Bartolomeo Vanzetti who were arrested in 1920 for a robbery and murder. The two men were immigrants from Italy who had been living in the US for many years by the time of the trial. The men also had radical, revolutionary ideas. Some people thought they might be communists.

The trial began in July 1921. Many Americans felt that the two men would be found guilty not because they were guilty of the robbery and murder, but because they were immigrants and had strong radical ideas about changing the US system.

Public opinion was divided: some Americans believed that anyone who wanted to change the whole USA political system was already guilty and should be hanged. Others believed that in a democracy all people should be free to believe what they want. Because of protest both at home and abroad, the trial dragged on for six years.

In his final statement on April 7, 1927, Vanzetti claimed that the trial had not been about murder, but rather his political ideas and where he came from:

SOURCE 3.6

I am suffering because I am a radical. Indeed I am a radical. I have suffered because I was an Italian. Indeed, I am an Italian.

On August 23, 1927, Sacco and Vanzetti were executed.

1921 New Immigration Laws.

1924 More cuts in immigration.

SOURCE 3.7

IMMIGRATION LAWS IN THE 1920s

By the 1920s several laws had restricted the flow of immigrants to the USA. A *quota system* was used. That meant that only so many immigrants from each country were allowed in to the USA.

For example, an immigration law passed in 1921 meant that only so many immigrants would be allowed in from each country in Europe. The law said that only 3% of each nationality living in the USA in 1910 would be allowed to enter the USA. In 1924 another immigration act set a total of 150 000 immigrants for each year and the proportion from each country was decided on the sizes of national groups in the USA at the time of the 1890 census. You should remember that up to 1890 most immigrants had come from countries such as Britain, Germany and Scandinavia.

The effect of both the 1921 and the 1924 Immigration Acts was to *discriminate* against people from Southeastern Europe and allow more immigrants from Northern Europe to enter the USA. In 1928 the balance was slightly altered when the Census of 1910, which accounted for more East Europeans, was used as the basis of the quotas.

In 1932 Franklin Roosevelt, the man who was about to become the next president of the USA, summed up the reasons why the USA no longer had an open door policy.

SOURCE 3.8

Our last frontier has long since been reached ... There is no safety valve in the form of a Western prairie ... We are not able to invite immigration from Europe to share our endless plenty.

Summary section

◆ In the nineteenth century the USA had an open door policy on immigration.

◆ An open door policy meant that almost anyone could go to the USA.

◆ By the 1920s the open door policy had ended.

◆ Laws stopped many immigrants entering the USA.

◆ Immigrants were blamed for many of the USA's problems in the 1920s.

QUESTION PRACTICE

SOURCE A Alistair Cook, *America*, page 310

The country was seized with the fear that the last great wave of immigration had brought the revolutionary infection with them.

1 Explain why the US government tried to limit immigration after 1918.

Outcome 2

SOURCE B

By the 1920s several laws had restricted the flow of immigrants to the USA. Only so many immigrants from each country were allowed in to the USA.

2 What did the USA do to limit immigration after 1918?

Outcome 1

QUESTION PRACTICE

For Intermediate 2 you will have to write some longer answers. They are called Extended Answers.

Your extended answer is worth 8 marks.

Why did attitudes towards immigration change in the 1920s?

Outcome 2

You will find advice on how to write an 8 mark answer on pages 118 and 119.

Since this is your first 8 mark essay you will also find advice about doing this question on pages 118 and 119.

BLACK AMERICANS – THE 'IN-MIGRANTS'

In this chapter you will find out:
- ◆ Black Americans moved north throughout the twentieth century
- ◆ they moved to find a better life
- ◆ Black Americans often found prejudice and persecution wherever they went.

At the beginning of the twentieth century Black people were not immigrants in the same sense as the people from Europe who flooded into the USA. For one thing Black people were really Black Americans. They were already 'citizens' of the USA. However, in some ways the reasons behind the migration of Black Americans were the same as for poor Europeans – the chance of a better life and a brighter future. One historian even referred to the move of thousands of Black Americans northwards as 'in-migration.'

THE MOVE NORTH

The migration of Black Americans to the north and midwest of the USA had been going on for some time but speeded up around 1914. At that time industries in the north were growing fast and were demanding cheap workers. As immigration from Europe slowed to a trickle through the 1920s, Black Americans were encouraged to head north. This was the chance that Black Americans had been awaiting since the end of the Civil War.

SOURCE 4.1 *Slum housing was common in the south as well as the north*

SOURCE 4.2 *Black Americans moved from the South to the major northern cities*

LIFE IN THE SOUTH

The Civil War which ended in 1865 had given Black Americans freedom in a legal sense. However, in the south, Black Americans were paid lower wages than White workers doing the same job. Less money was spent on education for Black Americans and they were often 'the last hired and the first fired.' As a well known guitarist and blues singer wrote:

SOURCE 4.3 *Many Black Americans simply walked north following the rail tracks which led to Chicago*

SOURCE 4.4 'Black, brown and White' by Big Bill Broonzy

If you're White, that's all right
If you're brown, stick around,
but if you're Black – get back, get back, get back!

In the Southern states of the USA 'native born' White Americans disliked and feared the Negroes. In the North the thousands of poor Whites looking for work and jobs saw Black Americans as unwelcome competition.

In the South, Black Americans were treated as second-class citizens. They could be beaten, kidnapped and killed and no White person in authority seemed to care.

By moving north, Black Americans saw a chance of a better life. However, when they arrived in the North, Black Americans found that they faced the same difficulties as the thousands of other immigrants. They were seen as uneducated and unskilled. Black workers were paid less than White workers, so the Black migrants were seen as a definite threat to the job security of unskilled White workers already in the North.

PROBLEMS IN THE NORTH

Black Americans had extra problems facing them. One of these was the fact that Black Americans had been slaves not so long ago. The result was that many Whites felt they were a superior race to Black Americans. The other problem was their skin colour. Black Americans were easily identified as 'different' and that made it easier to discriminate against them. The same was true of Asian immigrants on the west coast of the USA.

In the industrial cities of the North, Black Americans found themselves segregated, or divided and separated, into communities that would become known as ghettos. Black Americans were denied close links with the White communities. The separation of races in the schools and neighbourhoods helped to make Black American children grow up feeling inferior. Black Americans quickly learned that even though the North had fought to abolish slavery, Black Americans were still seen as being 'free' in a legal sense only. In the North many Black Americans still found *prejudice* and discrimination. However, it was still better than life in the South.

Migration to the North was a first step in the climb to improve the lives of many Black Americans – but it did not mean that they had found the American dream.

It was not impossible for a Black American to be a success in the USA, but it was not easy. Around 1920, Black Americans were able to grow and prosper only within their own communities.

CASE STUDY – TULSA, OKLAHOMA AND THE BLACK WALL STREET

At the turn of the century many Black Americans prospered within their own communities. Since they could not shop nor do business in the White community, they built their own stores, restaurants, and businesses. One area which was particularly prosperous was Tulsa, Oklahoma. Some of the wealthiest Black Americans lived there. Some people called it the Black Wall Street. The real Wall Street is in New York and is the heart of US business. In Tulsa, Oklahoma, there were hundreds of Black businesses throughout the city, but most were confined to one Black neighbourhood area in Tulsa.

THE TULSA RIOT

On May 21, 1921, the lives of the Black Americans in Tulsa changed forever. A Black man was accused of raping a White woman. White racist groups such as the Ku Klux Klan organised racist attacks. White Americans stormed into the Black community. The police helped the White attackers. In less than 12 hours, the large Black business district of Tulsa was completely destroyed. By June 1, 1921, 600 businesses, 21 churches, several schools and libraries, and the livelihoods of nearly 3,000 Black Americans had been wiped out.

SOURCE 4.5 *Racism and jealousy were the two main reasons for the attack on Black Wall Street*

The riot demonstrated the fine balance that existed between Black American progress and the constant threat of White discrimination, *persecution* and violence.

Summary section
- Black Americans usually faced even more problems than any other group of migrants.
- Some Black Americans became successful in the 1920s.
- Most Black Americans had to live with White prejudice and discrimination.

5 THE END OF SLAVERY – FREE AT LAST?

In this chapter you will find out:
- how and why states in the South made their own laws to make life difficult for Black Americans in the late nineteenth century
- what Jim Crow laws were
- how and why it was difficult for Black Americans to vote
- what 'Separate but Equal' means.

SOURCE 5.1 *Before and after the Civil War many Black Americans worked on cotton plantations*

Until 1863 most Black people in America were slaves. The White owners of slaves could buy and sell their slaves at any time. Slave families could be split up almost without warning. Most slaves worked on plantations.

THE END OF SLAVERY

Plantations were large farms that produced mostly cotton or tobacco. Plantation owners argued that if slavery was abolished the plantations would be ruined. Most of these plantations were in the southern states of the USA. A more common word for the southern states of the USA is the 'South'. In 1861 the American Civil War began. One of the reasons for the war was the question of slavery. The northern states – the North – did not want slavery. The South, however, did. In 1863 slavery was abolished and when the North won the Civil War it looked as if Black people would be 'Free At Last'.

Black people were even more hopeful of a better life in 1868 when a change was made to the *Constitution* (a word for a set of rules which say how the USA should be governed) which said that Black people had the right to freedom and to be treated by law in the same way as White people. In 1870 another change to the Constitution, called officially the Fifteenth *Amendment* , gave Black American adult males the right to vote. The Fifteenth Amendment also said that nobody should lose their right to vote because of their colour or race.

THE BEGINNING OF JIM CROW

The South was determined to keep control over the Black population. They made new laws in their own states called Jim Crow laws. The name Jim Crow is just a general name for all sorts of laws which made sure Black and White people were kept separate and that Black people were denied their legal rights. The government of the USA is called the *Federal government* but the USA is a collection of 50 separate states. Each state has its own state government which can pass its own laws affecting life within the state. Most Jim Crow Laws were passed between 1870 and 1900. Here are some real examples of Jim Crow laws.

SOURCE 5.2 *Jim Crow laws*

The State of Florida
All marriages between a White person and a Negro are hereby forever prohibited.

The State of Georgia
It shall be unlawful for coloured people to use any park for the use and enjoyment of White persons … and unlawful for any White person to use any park for the use and benefit of coloured persons.

The State of Mississippi
Separate schools shall be maintained for the children of the White and coloured races.

The State of Alabama
Every employer of White or Negro males shall provide for such White or Negro males separate toilet facilities.

The State of Louisiana
There will be a separate building … on separate ground for the admission, care, instruction, and support of all blind persons of the coloured or Black race.

SOURCE 5.3 *Even drinking water was segregated*

The effect of Jim Crow laws was to create a segregated society. Many White southerners said that purpose of Jim Crow laws was to keep Black and White people apart. They also said that segregation just meant that Black and White people would have separate but equal facilities. Most Black people disagreed with the 'separate but equal' claim. They agreed that Jim Crow laws kept the races apart but Black Americans claimed facilities such as rest rooms and railway carriages were seldom separate *and* equal.

JIM CROW BECOMES RESPECTABLE – SEPARATE BUT EQUAL, 1896

Although the Federal government did not like states ignoring Federal laws about Black rights, little was done to stop Jim Crow laws spreading. In 1896 a decision of the Supreme Court made Jim Crow laws fully legal and made life even more difficult for Black people in America. The Supreme Court is the most important law court in America and what they decided in 1896 affected race relations in the USA for the next 60 years.

In 1892 a Black man called Homer Plessy objected to having to move from his seat on a train just because it was reserved for White people. Plessy was arrested and eventually the case went to the Supreme Court. Plessy argued that the Jim Crow laws broke Federal law and was against the Constitution of the USA. Plessy lost his case. In 1896 the Supreme Court decided it was acceptable for Black and White people to be segregated as long as equal facilities were provided for each race. The Supreme Court said:

SOURCE 5.4

Laws which keep the races apart do not mean that one race is better or worse than the other.

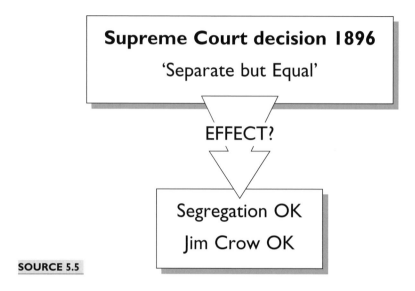

SOURCE 5.5

Black people were saddened by the decision of the Supreme Court. They knew that White southern states were unlikely to provide equal services. Black people said that the decision of the Supreme Court made it legal in the USA to discriminate against them and they were right.

SOURCE 5.6

The realities of Jim Crow were harsh. Wherever Black people lived or travelled in the south they were faced with the humiliation of seeing doors that were open to White people legally closed to them: restaurant and motel doors, movie house doors ... the public parks, pools, beaches ... were all closed. Or they would find two sets of doors, two kinds of facilities from drinking fountains to schools. One set of doors was White the other was Black, one set was clean and well cared for ... the other was usually broken, neglected by the White authorities, shamefully unequal.

After 1896 more Jim Crow laws spread across the South. Segregation became the usual way of life in the South and did not start to change until 1954 when the Supreme Court made another decision which you will find out about later.

Even the President of the USA said:

SOURCE 5.7 President Wilson, 1916

Segregation is not humiliating and is a benefit for you Black gentlemen.

Chapter summary

The effect of Jim Crow

- After the Civil War southern states were determined not to allow Black Americans to be free
- Jim Crow laws kept White and Black people separate
- Black Americans were easily prevented from voting
- The word which means keeping White and Black apart is segregation
- Most White people in the south believed that 'separate but equal' was a good idea
- Most Black Americans believed that separate but equal really meant separate and unequal
- The decision of the Supreme Court in 1896 meant that segregation spread all over the United States

BLACK PEOPLE AND THE RIGHT TO VOTE

As early as 1867 Black men who had once been slaves were given the right to vote, but in the years that followed states made it harder and harder for Black people to do so. By 1900 very few Black people in the South were able to vote. If they couldn't vote they could not elect politicians to fight against Jim Crow laws. How did the states manage to stop Black people voting?

To vote in the USA you have to register. Many southern states made up a series of rules (called voting qualifications) which made it difficult for Black Americans to vote. For example in some states people had to pay a poll tax. The tax rate was set so high that most Black people could not afford to pay. Since they did not pay the tax they could not vote.

In other states Black men had to take literacy tests which usually meant reading out a difficult document in front of a white listener who judged if it had been read well enough and if the reader really understood what he was reading. Not surprisingly, most Black men who were brave enough to take the test were failed – and so could not vote. Even more simply, Black men who went to register to vote were threatened and beaten up. The result was that by 1900 very few Black men voted – despite the Federal Law of 1870 which gave all Black men the vote.

SOURCE 5.8 An Alabama politician, 1900

We take away the Nigra's votes to help them. They don't understand politics. It makes their life easier. We know what is best for them.

State	Year	Black people with the right to vote
Alabama	1900	180,000
	1902	3,000

QUESTION PRACTICE

Look at the photograph in this chapter of men at a drinking fountain.

1 Explain why the drinking fountain is labelled 'Colored'.

Outcome 2

2 Describe how Jim Crow laws discriminated against Black Americans.

Outcome 1

SOURCE A is by William Mahoney, a man travelling in the South in the 1960s.

I saw a modern rest station with gleaming counters and picture windows labelled 'White'. A small wooden shack beside it was tagged 'colored'. The colored waiting room was filthy, in need of repair and overcrowded.

QUESTION PRACTICE

SOURCE B was written by an old Black farmer in 1920.

I remember my grandaddy telling me how he felt he was 'free at last' after the civil war. 'Free at last boy', he said, 'thanks to these northern laws'. He died a few years ago. He knew he had been fooled. Jim Crow broke his spirit.

SOURCE C is from a diary kept by a White woman in 1920.

My grandmother told me that freeing the slaves was the ruination of the South. Our plantations lost money and worst of all nigra folks (Black people) walked the streets as if they were the equals of White folks. Something had to be done – I thank the Lord for good old Jim Crow.

3 Compare the opinions of Sources B and C about the treatment of Black Americans after the Civil War.

Outcome 3

6

FEAR, TERROR AND LYNCHINGS

In this chapter you will find out:
◆ what was meant by lynching and lynch law
◆ that it was difficult for black people to find justice in the South.

Jim Crow laws and restriction on Black people's right to vote were ways of maintaining White power over Black people, but there was another way – fear. A Civil Rights worker reported:

SOURCE 6.1

A Negro in the South who tried to vote might lose his job or be beaten up. When a man was asked why he didn't vote he said, 'I don't want my throat cut.'

LYNCH LAW

'Lynching' was the word used to describe a variety of murders, tortures and punishments given to Black Americans. Lynching meant Black people being whipped, hanged or even burned alive by a mob who believed the Black person had done something wrong.

In 1920 a newspaper reported a lynching:

SOURCE 6.2

The Negro was chained to the tree stump, beaten and then castrated. The fire was lit and a hundred men and women, young and old, joined hands and danced around the burning Negro. That night a big party was held in a nearby barn.

Many Black Americans were afraid of being lynched. Lynchings were common.

SOURCE 6.3 *1952 was the first year when no lynchings were reported*

Date	Number of lynchings
1882	42
1887	70
1892	161
1897	123
1903	84
1910	67
1915	56
1921	51

SOURCE 6.4 *This photo was used as part of an NAACP anti-lynching campaign. Read the words underneath.*

Do not look at the Negro.

His earthly problems are ended.

Instead, look at the seven WHITE children who gaze at this gruesome spectacle.

Is it horror or gloating on the face of the neatly dressed seven-year-old girl on the right?

Is the tiny four-year-old on the left old enough, one wonders, to comprehend the barbarism her elders have perpetrated?

Rubin Stacy, the Negro, who was lynched at Fort Lauderdale, Florida, on July 19, 1935, for 'threatening and frightening a white woman,' suffered PHYSICAL torture for a few short hours. But what psychological havoc is being wrought in the minds of the white children?

SOURCE 6.5 *The Scottsboro boys discovered how difficult it was for Black Americans to find justice*

'Lynch law' was a phrase that meant a group of people, usually White, would decide themselves that a Black person was guilty of a 'crime' and would then punish that person. The point about a lynching is that it was illegal. There was no trial, no defence and no judge. Yet little was done to stop lynching.

THE SCOTTSBORO BOYS

In the 1930s a famous case that became world news showed just how difficult it was for Black Americans to find justice in the South.

On March 25, 1931, nine young men between the ages of 13 and 21 rode a freight train away from their home town of Chattanooga in the state of Tennessee. At least one of the nine young Black men, Eugene Williams, thought that the idea of leaving his home seemed like a good one. 'If I leave home,' he said to his mother, 'it will mean one less mouth to feed.'

By the end of the day, Williams was one of the nine young Black males taken off the train by a sheriff's gang and charged with raping two White girls.

This was the beginning of a long legal case which showed up the racism, prejudice and discrimination that existed in parts of the USA in the 1930s.

The case dragged on for nine years.

GUILTY?

The trial was known as the trial of the Scottsboro Boys. Scottsboro was the town in Alabama where they were tried for the first time. The nine boys were charged with attacking two young White women. One of the women was a town prostitute. The boys all said they were not guilty but their not guilty statements were quickly rejected by an all White jury. Eight of the nine boys were sentenced to death on April 9, 1931.

In the South in the 1930s it was almost automatic for any Black American to be found guilty if they were accused of a crime by a White person.

The Scottsboro boys faced a legal system that was full of racism and prejudice. Their legal defence was in the hands of a local lawyer who had been given no time or help in preparing a defence.

A LYNCHING PARTY

On the day of the trial 10 000 White demonstrators came in to Scottsboro to pressurise the jury. On the day of the trial a crowd gathered outside the courthouse and staged a demonstration complete with a band playing 'There'll be a hot time in the old town tonight.' The crowd wanted the Black boys to be found guilty. Perhaps the crowd was hoping for a lynching party.

SUPPORT FOR THE BOYS

In other areas of America there were protests in support of the Scottsboro boys. Just one day after the death sentences were passed, the first big demonstration was held in Harlem, a Black area of New York. Money was found from various groups to pay for a better legal defence.

There was even a lot of support for the Scottsboro boys from countries far from the USA. Demonstrations in support of the boys were held in German towns. World famous people such as Albert Einstein signed a petition demanding the release of the nine young men. Eventually, supporters of the boys had a new ally. Her name was Ruby Bates. She was one of the women the boys were supposed to have raped but she said the attack had never happened.

A NEW TRIAL

Finally, on November 8, 1932, Judge Hawkins agreed to have new trials for all nine boys but once again the boys faced an all-White jury. Once again the people of the town made it clear they wanted the Black boys to die.

The trials of the nine boys dragged on for several years and eventually charges were dropped against five of the nine. The other four were retried and convicted; three were later paroled, and the fourth, Patterson, escaped.

The trial of the Scottsboro Boys raised awareness all over America of the bad treatment of Black Americans in the South.

Twenty years later, in 1955, the murder of 14 year old Emmett Till showed that it was still almost impossible for Black Americans to get fair treatment from the law in the South.

THE MURDER OF EMMETT TILL

SOURCE 6.6 Extract from *The Death of Emmett Till* by Bob Dylan

'Twas down in Mississippi not so long ago,
When a young boy from Chicago town stepped through a Southern door.
This boy's dreadful tragedy I can still remember well,
The color of his skin was Black and his name was Emmett Till.

In August 1955, a fourteen year old boy called Emmett Till went to visit relatives near Money, Mississippi. Emmett Till thought he knew about segregation because he went to a Black only school in a poor area of Chicago. What Emmett did not know about was the severe segregation and prejudices of people in Mississippi.

'BYE BABY'

When he arrived in Money, Mississippi, Emmett showed some local boys a picture of a White girl who was one of his friends back home. Emmett said she was his girlfriend. The other boys were amazed because no Black boy ever went out with a White girl in Mississippi. One of Emmett's friends said, 'Hey, there's a White girl in that store there. I bet you won't go in there and talk to her.' Emmett went in, bought some bubble gum and as he left, he said 'Bye baby' to Carolyn Bryant, the wife of the store owner.

KIDNAPPED AT NIGHT

A few days later, two men drove up to the house of Emmett's uncle, in the middle of the night. One of the men was Roy Bryant, the husband of the girl Emmett had spoken to. The two men grabbed Emmett and drove away with him. Three days later, Emmett Till's body was found in the Tallahatchie River. One eye was gouged out, and his crushed-in head had a bullet in it. The corpse was nearly unrecognisable. The only way that Emmett could be recognised was by an initialled ring that he wore.

At first, local Whites as well as Black Americans were horrified by the crime. Bryant and his friend were arrested for kidnapping even before Emmett's body was found, and no local White lawyers would defend the men. Newspapers reported that all 'decent' people were disgusted with the murder and said that 'justice would be done.'

A BATTERED BODY WAS FOUND

The Emmett Till case quickly attracted national attention. Mamie Bradley, Emmett's mother, asked for her son's body to be taken back to Chicago. When it arrived, she was not sure the body was her son because it had been so beaten up. Emmett's mother was sickened but also angry. She said:

SOURCE 6.7

Have you ever sent a loved son on vacation and had him returned to you in a pine box, so horribly battered and water-logged that someone needs to tell you this sickening sight is your son – lynched?'

Emmett's mother insisted that her son lay in an open coffin so that local people and newspaper photographers could see what had happened to him. Over four days, thousands of people saw Emmett's body. Many more people across the country were shocked by pictures that appeared in magazines. All across the USA Black Americans were demanding that 'something be done in Mississippi now.' The NAACP said that Emmett had been lynched.

DON'T INTERFERE WITH SOUTHERN JUSTICE!

Whites in Mississippi resented the Northern criticism of the 'barbarity of segregation'. Five lawyers said they would defend Milam and Bryant, and people who had at first said that the murder was awful now began supporting the accused murderers. The two men went on trial in a segregated courthouse in Sumner, Mississippi on September 19, 1955. The jury was all White and very few people would speak up against the two men accused of the murder.

NOT GUILTY!

At that time in Mississippi, it was unheard of for a Black to publicly accuse a White of committing a crime. Finally, Emmett's sixty-four year old uncle was asked if he could point out the men who had kidnapped Emmett. He stood, pointed to Milam and Bryant, and said 'There they are'. After Emmett's uncle had spoken out, other Black neighbours gave evidence against the accused men. All the Black witnesses had to be taken out of the state and hidden in a place of safety. In the end, all the evidence against Milam and Bryant made no difference. The all-White jury considered the evidence for just over an hour, then gave a 'not guilty' verdict. The jury foreman later explained, 'I feel the state failed to prove that the body really was that of Emmett Till'. He also said the not guilty verdict would have been passed more quickly if the jury had not stopped to drink lemonade before returning to the court.

THE IMPORTANCE OF EMMETT TILL'S DEATH

The Emmett Till case had a big effect on the Civil Rights Movement. The North became aware of the full horror of segregation and persecution of Black Americans in the South. In the words of Mamie Bradley (Emmett's mother), 'Two months ago I had a nice apartment in Chicago. I had a good job. I had a son. When something happened to the Negroes in the South I said, "That's their business, not mine." ' Black Americans, in the North as well as in the South, would not easily forget the murder of Emmett Till.

After the murder of Emmett Till, the Chicago Defender (a newspaper) printed this comment about justice in the South:

SOURCE 6.8

How long must we wait for the Federal government to act? The Department of Justice seems to explore its law books for reasons why it can't offer protection of a Negroe's life. There has never been a congressional (Federal government) investigation of lynching or any of the other abuses suffered by Negroes.

Chapter summary
- Many Black Americans in the South lived in fear and terror.
- Many Black Americans were murdered by White mobs.
- It was very difficult for Black Americans to find justice in the South.

7 THE KU KLUX KLAN

In this chapter you will find out:
◆ what the Ku Klux Klan was
◆ why the Ku Klux Klan got away with terrorism against Black Americans.

The history of the world is the fight for survival of the White race. Either we win or we die. The Klan will not die.
Hiram Wesley Evans, Imperial Wizard, Ku Klux Klan.

SOURCE 7.1

SOURCE 7.2 *The Ku Klux Klan scared people by using violence and dressing like ghosts*

The Ku Klux Klan was, and still is, a secret terrorist organisation which started in the southern states following the American Civil War. It died down in the late nineteenth century but in 1915 a new Klan was established.

HOW WAS THE KLAN ORGANISED?

◆ The Klan was known as the Invisible Empire.
◆ The Klan was led by a Grand Wizard of the Empire.
◆ Local Klan organisations were called klaverns.
◆ All members had to be native-born Americans, White, Protestant males, 16 years of age or older.
◆ No Black Americans, Roman Catholics or Jews were allowed to be in the Klan.
◆ Klansmen wore robes or sheets and masks topped with pointed hoods.

WHAT DID THE KLAN DO?

◆ Klansmen often burned large crosses on hillsides and near the homes of people they wished to frighten.
◆ If their victims still would not do what the Klansmen wanted them to do, victims might be kidnapped, whipped, mutilated, or murdered.
◆ Masked Klansmen marched through the streets of towns and cities carrying posters threatening various persons with punishment and warning others to leave town.
◆ The Klan *lynched* many Black Americans.

WHAT DID THE KU KLUX KLAN BELIEVE IN?

◆ The Klansmen believed that Black Americans were inferior human beings.
◆ The Klan were against any Civil Rights laws.
◆ The Klan was also against Catholics, Jews and even divorced women.
◆ The Klan justified its actions by saying they were protecting 'the American way of life'.

Until 1920 the Klan had little influence, but after 1920 the Klan grew quickly.

WHY DID SUPPORT FOR THE KLAN INCREASE?

◆ Unemployment was growing.
◆ New immigrants were flooding into the USA.
◆ Black Americans were moving north competing with poor Whites for houses and jobs.
◆ Poor Whites saw the Klan as their protectors.

The Klan attacked any group they called 'un-American'. That meant any group of people which the Klan believed was threatening traditional American life. In the 1920s all non-Protestants, new immigrants and Black Americans became targets for Klan attacks. The Klan used fear to stop Black Americans registering to vote. They did not accept Black people as equal citizens. In the South the Klan's main targets were Black Americans. An old farm worker remembered:

SOURCE 7.4

If coloured folks tried to better themselves the Ku Klux Klan would come and murder them. When voting time came round the Ku Klux would be waiting outside the voting place. No coloured folks would try to vote.

Many Black people in the southern states of the USA lived in isolated communities and were easy targets for the KKK.

SOURCE 7.5

The sight of crosses burning meant the Klan was out and looking for targets to hit. Many a Black family living in isolated farms shook with fear until the morning.

SOURCE 7.3 *The Ku Klux Klan became popular in small towns across America*

HOW IMPORTANT WAS THE KLAN?

It's difficult to know how many members the Klan had because it was a secret organisation. One estimate of Klan membership, made in 1924, when the Klan was at the peak of its strength, was as high as three million.

The other point to remember is that the Klan did have important friends. In the 1920s the Klan was powerful enough to hold large marches through Washington, the capital city of the USA.

It seemed as if nothing could be done to stop the terror tactics of the Klan. Although the Klan was popular with some Americans, the organisation was still illegal. It used terrorist tactics but few Klansmen were arrested and in some communities the Klan was helped by local officials.

SOURCE 7.6 *The Ku Klux Klan wanted to give the impression that it was a patriotic, large organisation with friends in high places*

SOURCE 7.7 Robert F. Williams

Each time the Klan came on a raid they were led by police cars. We appealed to the President of the United States to investigate the police. All our appeals were in vain.

WHAT DO YOU THINK?

Why did the Klan, an illegal organisation, seem to be immune from legal actions to stop it?

As the *Civil Rights movement* gathered speed in the late 1950s, the Klan continued to oppose the Civil Rights movement and was believed to be involved in many incidents of racial violence, intimidation, and bombings. After the US Civil Rights Act of 1964 when Black Americans were given full legal equality the Klan became more popular and membership increased. By the end of the twentieth century the Klan still existed and in the late 1990s was thought to be involved in the brutal murder of a Black American in Texas.

Chapter Summary
- The Ku Klux Klan was created to defend 'the American Way of Life'.
- In the South the main target of the KKK were Black Americans.
- The KKK had important friends in local politics and in the local police.
- The KKK literally got away with murder.

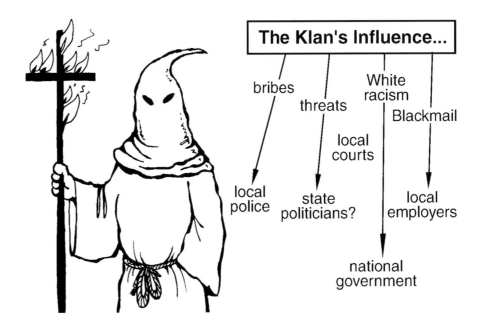

The Klan's Influence...

bribes — local police
threats — state politicians?
local courts
White racism — national government
Blackmail — local employers

SOURCE 7.8

QUESTION PRACTICE   *i1*

Source A was part of a booklet published in 1966 by a friend of Martin Luther King. It refers to events in the 1950s.

SOURCE A

Ever since the Civil Rights movement began the leaders have received death threats over the phone and through the mail. Police joined in the harassment. Phones were tapped. One man, the Rev. Charles Billups, was arrested. Later he was tied to a tree and beaten by the Ku Klux Klan.

I How useful is Source A as evidence that fear and terror were used against the Civil Rights movement?

Outcome 3

Source B was written by a Civil Rights campaigner in the 1950s

SOURCE B

Each time the Klan came on a raid they were led by police cars.

2 Why did some people believe that 'little was done to stop lynchings'? Use Source B and your own knowledge to answer this question.

Outcome 2

QUESTION PRACTICE   *i2*

8 mark question

This task is a revision exercise. You must use most of the information you have gathered from the last two chapters in your answer. Try to write an answer of at least one A4 page.

In what ways were the lives of Black Americans made difficult in the late nineteenth and early twentieth centuries?

You are asked about 'the late nineteenth and early twentieth centuries' so your information must be about that time period.

The following list should remind you of the main points that should be in your answer:

Jim Crow Laws, segregation and the Supreme Court decision of 1896, the way that Black Americans were prevented from voting and finally the fear and terror of lynching and the Ku Klux Klan.

Look at the advice about writing 8 mark answers at the end of this book.

8

FIGHT FOR THE RIGHT? – EARLY CIVIL RIGHTS CAMPAIGNS

In this chapter you will find out:
◆ what the NAACP was
◆ who Marcus Garvey, Booker T. Washington and W. E. B. Du Bois were
◆ black leaders had very different views about how to improve the lives of Black Americans.

In the years following 1896 the Black population of America did not just accept segregation and discrimination as 'normal'. Several organisations were formed to help improve the lives of Black Americans. There were three main leaders who had very different ideas about how to win Civil Rights These differences can be summed up in three questions.
◆ Should Black Americans fight for the right to be treated fairly?
◆ Or should they persuade White people to treat them equally?
◆ Or should Black Americans denied equal treatment simply leave the USA and start fresh somewhere else?

WHAT DO YOU THINK?

As you read this chapter think about this:
   If you had been a Black American in the early 1920s which of the three leaders described in this chapter would you have supported? Why? Why would you not have supported the others?

THE NAACP

The National Association for the Advancement of Coloured People, called the NAACP for short, was founded in 1909. It is the oldest and largest US civil-rights organisation. The purpose of the NAACP was to campaign for the rights of Black Americans.

Since its beginning the NAACP has used legal action in its fight to improve employment, housing, voting, and education.

The first leader of the NAACP was W. E. B. Du Bois. In 1895 Du Bois was the first Black to be awarded a degree from Harvard University. Du Bois supported complete racial equality and disagreed with the ideas of Booker T. Washington.

BOOKER T. WASHINGTON HAD DIFFERENT IDEAS FROM DU BOIS

Booker T. Washington was born in 1856. He was the son of a slave. He became well known as a teacher and made a Black school in Tuskegee, Alabama into a big success. The school specialised in industrial and agricultural training of Black Americans. All this fitted in with Washington's main belief which was that Black Americans should be trained for trades before fighting for Civil Rights and equality. In the early 1900s he argued that Black people would advance only if they were educated.

SOURCE 8.1 *W. E. B. Du Bois*
We are Americans. We claim for ourselves every single right that belongs to a freeborn American ... and until we get these rights we will never cease to protest

SOURCE 8.2 *Booker T. Washington: 'You should stop demanding equal rights. Education is the answer. Show White people that you can work hard and save for the future and then they will see that the Black man is a respectable person. Then we will be granted our rights.'*

White Americans were pleased when Washington made a speech which said that Black people should accept their inferior position in America for the present and to try to improve themselves by hard work and education. On the other hand, Black leaders such as Du Bois totally refused to accept that Black Americans were in any way inferior to White Americans.

MARCUS GARVEY SUPPORTED BLACK NATIONALISM

Marcus Garvey believed all Black Americans should return to Africa and start their own self governing country there.

In New York City, Garvey began his Universal Negro Improvement Association (UNIA) and started a weekly newspaper, the Negro World. Garvey encouraged American Black Americans to be proud of their race and preached their return to Africa, their ancestral homeland. Garvey even started his own steamship company called the Black Star Line to provide steamship transportation to Africa. In 1920 Garvey claimed to have two million members for the UNIA. Garvey became less important when he was jailed for fraud in 1925 but Black historians agree that his 'Back to Africa' movement led on to ideas in the 1960s.

SOURCE 8.3 *Marcus Garvey: 'Why should we try to fit into a White world? Why should we ask to be given Civil Rights? Black is beautiful! Up, you mighty race, you can do what you set out to do! Europe for the Europeans, Asia for the Asians and Africa for the Africans! I say back to Africa!'*

Chapter Summary

◆ By the early 1900s there were three main Black leaders.

◆ These leaders were called W. E. B. Du Bois, Marcus Garvey and Booker T. Washington.

◆ They had different views on how to improve the lives of Black Americans.

QUESTION PRACTICE

i1

Source A was said in 1906 by one of the founders of the NAACP.

SOURCE A

Yes we want our children educated. We also want the right to vote and we want it now. We want segregation to end. We will never cease to protest until we get our rights.

1 What were the aims of the NAACP?   *Outcome 1*

SOURCE B is about a speech made by Booker T. Washington in 1895.

He said that Black people should not let their anger at the way white people treat them stop them from working hard and getting a training in a good job. Protests are a waste of time. If Black people worked hard and improved their lives they could show that they deserved better treatment.

2 Are Sources A and B useful evidence about early campaigns to win Black Americans Civil Rights? *Outcome 3*

QUESTION PRACTICE

3 What are the similarities and differences between the ideas of Booker T. Washington and the NAACP?

Outcome 3

9

PRESSURE FOR CHANGE – 'THE GREAT MIGRATION'

In this chapter you will find out:
◆ what is meant by the 'Great Migration'
◆ what effect the Great Migration had on Black Americans.

Although the ideas of Garvey, Du Bois and Booker T. Washington appealed to many Black Americans, all these leaders seemed to promise something better in the future. Black Americans wanted a better life now! There was little sign of any improvements in the South so many Black Americans decided to leave the South and head North.

In the late years of the nineteenth century Black Americans began moving from their homes in the rural South to Northern industrial cities. These migrants looked for better wages and a better life away from segregation and fear.

SOURCE 9.1 *Black people had many incentives to move North*

THE MOVE NORTH

The 'Great Migration' increased dramatically in the years between about 1910 and the early 1920s. About 500,000 Black people moved north in this period, mainly because there were many unskilled factory jobs available during World War One.

Migration north continued steadily through the 1920s and 1930s but the 1940s saw the largest Black migration from the South. During World War Two, just like in World War One, factories in the north needed as many workers as they could get. Once again thousands of Black people migrated north. In the 1940s nearly one million Black Americans made the move from South to North. By 1950, for the first time, a third of all Black Americans lived outside the South. By the 1960s over six million southern Black people had migrated from the South to the North.

RACE TENSIONS IN THE NORTH

The 'Great Migration' of Black Americans to the north may have made some problems worse. Competition for housing and jobs between White and Black workers showed segregation and discrimination existed in the North as well as the South.

Black ghettos grew up. When Black Americans arrived from the South they were often poor. They looked for cheap housing and cheap housing tended to be in run down areas. These poor areas became known as Black ghettos. There was no official segregation in the North but in the northern cities the races were segregated by the area in which they lived.

RACE RIOTS

Race riots were often linked to the growth of northern cities and the large increases of their immigrant White and Black populations. Competition over jobs and housing increased tension. The riots usually started as small arguments between individuals but then spread quickly. The White police usually sided with the White rioters. Often Federal troops had to be brought in to restore order.

The East St. Louis riot in 1917 is an example of a small dispute that blew up into a riot. Two White police detectives were shot by Black youths. In retaliation a White mob invaded the Black area of the town. Black women and children were beaten and a number of Black men were lynched while the police watched. This riot left 50 dead.

The Chicago riot of 1919 started when several Black youths using a 'Whites Only' beach near Chicago. A row broke out and one Black youth was hit by a stone and drowned. The police refused to arrest the White man who the Black youths said had thrown the stone. The Black youths then attacked the police. That evening gangs of White teenagers began to attack Black Americans in Chicago. The city erupted in a five-day race riot that ended with 38 deaths, 537 serious injuries, and large scale destruction.

Later, during World War Two, a riot in Detroit resulted in 34 deaths, hundreds of injuries and whole areas destroyed.

The riots showed that race problems did not only belong in the South. Federal politicians had to wake up to the fact that prejudice, discrimination and segregation existed in the North as well as in the South.

HOW THE MOVE NORTH HELPED MANY BLACK AMERICANS

On the other hand there were benefits of the Great Migration. In the Harlem area of New York the 'Harlem Renaissance' of the 1920s and 1930s encouraged a very positive image of Black people. A new pride in Black culture led to a boom in Black music, art and a sense of pride in being Black. Jazz music, which many people say is one of the roots of today's rock and pop, grew out of the new sense of identity.

The Great Migration opened up a brighter future for many Black Americans and in the long run might have helped to force the Federal government to do something about the 'Race Problem'.

Chapter summary
- Thousands of Black Americans migrated to the Northern cities between 1900 and 1950.
- The Great Migration had good and bad effects: for example race riots were bad but better jobs and wages were good.
- Tension and riots in Northern cities showed that segregation and discrimination were not just Southern problems.

10

PRESSURE FOR CHANGE – WORLD WAR TWO AND EXECUTIVE ORDER 8802

In this chapter you will find out:
◆ why A. Philip Randolph was important
◆ what the Double V campaign was
◆ why World War Two was important to the cause of Civil Rights.

In many ways World War Two was an important turning point in the campaign Civil Rights in the USA. Black soldiers talked about 'the Double-V campaign'.

SOURCE 10.1

The Double-V campaign meant Victory in the war AND Victory for Civil Rights back home in the USA.

Many historians agree that World War Two planted seeds that grew into the Civil Rights movement of the 1950s and 60s. Much of the credit for sowing those seeds should go to A. Philip Randolph.

A. PHILIP RANDOLPH

During the Black migration to the northern cities, sleeping car porters on the railroads were an important link between North and South. Since their work took them across the country, porters could carry news between Black communities in the rural South and those in Northern cities. The president of the Brotherhood of Sleeping Car Porters, a mainly Black trade union, was A. Philip Randolph.

SOURCE 10.2 *A. Philip Randolph*

A MARCH ON WASHINGTON

During World War Two, A. Philip Randolph threatened a mass protest march in Washington unless discrimination in defence industry jobs and in the armed forces was ended. In 1941, A. Philip Randolph and other Black leaders met with the President. Randolph gave him a list of complaints about the lack of Civil Rights of Black Americans, and demanded that the President make a special order (called an *executive order*) to stop job discrimination in the defence industry. In total, Randolph made three demands:

1 Immediate end to segregation and discrimination in federal government jobs.
2 An end to segregation of the armed forces.
3 Government support for an end to discrimination and segregation in all jobs in America.

President Roosevelt tried to convince Randolph that change must come slowly but Randolph and the other Black leaders would not back down. Millions of jobs were being created in preparation for war (the USA did not join World War Two until December 1941). Because of widespread discrimination, however, very few Black Americans were getting any of the new jobs. Randolph said he was prepared to bring '*ten, twenty, fifty thousand Negroes on the White House lawn*' if their demands were not met.

FDR GIVES IN

The President, called Franklin Delano Roosevelt (or FDR for short), had been trying to drum up American support for a war against Hitler. Part of FDR's campaign methods were to explain the horror of Hitler's racist policy against Jews and other minorities in Europe. FDR needed Black soldiers to fight in the US armed forces but a march on Washington would be very embarrassing to the President since it would remind the American public of the racism that existed in the USA.

Eventually Roosevelt decided to give Randolph some of what he wanted and issued Executive Order 8802:

SOURCE 10.3 *Black soldiers fought in the name of freedom in Europe, but were denied it back home*

SOURCE 10.4

There shall be no discrimination in the employment of workers in defence industries and in Government, because of race, creed, color, or national origin.

Roosevelt also established the Fair Employment Practices Committee to investigate incidents of discrimination.

As it turned out, the new order did not end discrimination since employers found ways around the rule but discrimination in defence industry jobs was ended. However that was more likely a result of the demand for workers as war time production grew quickly. The second of Randolph's demands was not met. Segregation in the armed forces continued.

RACE TENSION INCREASES

There was also serious racial tension during the war. As more and more people crowded into towns which had lots of factories making weapons, competition for housing and jobs resulted in race riots.

In Detroit, 25 Black and 9 White people were killed before federal troops restored law and order.

In 1943 in Harlem, New York, five Black people died in the riots.

In the South there were outbreaks of violent protest also. There were up to 75 lynchings reported during the war.

THE IMPORTANCE OF WORLD WAR TWO FOR BLACK AMERICANS

The first small seed that was planted during World War Two was the creation of an organisation called **CORE.** The Congress of Racial Equality (CORE) was founded in 1942. It was the beginning of a mass movement for Civil Rights. Although early CORE membership was mainly northern and White, you will find out that the organisation played a big part in the Civil Rights protests of the 1950 and 1960s. Secondly, some Black Americans who belonged to the Nation of Islam refused to serve in the US armed forces. They believed in complete separation of the races and did not think it was right that Black soldiers should fight for White America. You'll read about the Nation of Islam later in this book. Their demands for separation echoed the aims of Marcus Garvey and can still be heard in the policies of Black leaders in the 1990s such as Louis Farrakhan.

In conclusion, many Civil Rights protests made during World War Two were important in showing where Black protest had come from and also where it was going.

CIVIL RIGHTS AFTER THE WAR

In the late 1940s there were some signs of improvement in race relations. There were also signs that nothing much had changed.

In 1947, Jackie Robinson joined the Brooklyn Dodgers to become the first Black American to play major league baseball.

The new US President, Harry Truman, tried to improve Civil Rights but his efforts had mixed results. Truman tried to end segregation in the armed forces, but the Army remained segregated until well into the 1950s.

One of Truman's proposed new laws showed just how much racism there still was in the USA. Truman suggested a new law that would make lynching a federal crime but it was rejected. Southern politicians still wanted to rule by fear and the rope.

The end of the war saw many protests about segregation and discrimination and the right to vote. However it would be wrong to think that Civil Rights protests really only started in the 1950s. Black Americans had been campaigning for Civil Rights for a long time before that.

The historian Dr Neil Wynn says:

SOURCE 10.5

If there was a Negro revolution in the 1950s and 60s it was a revolution born out of frustrated expectations: those expectations had developed in the previous decades and so too had the basis for the new organisations and new forms of protest which dominated the 1960s. The events of 1955–56 suggest strong elements of continuity with the preceding decades.

To put it more simply, protests and organisations that started before World War Two eventually led to the more organised Civil Rights movement of the 1950s and 1960s. As one Black American soldier said, 'After the end of the war, we just kept on fighting. It's just that simple.'

Chapter summary
- A. Philip Randolph was an important leader who persuaded the US President to make improvements in the treatment of Black Americans.
- World War Two made many Black Americans question why they were fighting for freedom abroad but still had to suffer discrimination and prejudice in America.
- Black soldiers supported the Double V campaign – victory against their enemies abroad and at home.

QUESTION PRACTICE

SOURCE A

	1890s	1960s
% of Black Americans living in the south	90.3%	10%
% of Black Americans living in the north	9.7%	90%

1 Describe the effects of the 'Great Migration'   *Outcome 1*

SOURCE B   is from 'The Eyes on the Prize', a book about the Civil Rights campaign.

By the time the war ended in 1945 it was clear that nothing at home would ever be quite the same again where the Black struggle for freedom and justice was concerned.

2 Why did World War Two cause important changes in Black attitudes to Civil Rights?   *Outcome 2*

QUESTION PRACTICE

This task is a revision exercise.

You must write an answer of at least one A4 page. This is your question:

How and why had the attitudes of Black Americans to Civil Rights changed before 1950?

Your answer should include the following:

The NAACP; the campaign of Booker T. Washington; the ideas of Marcus Garvey; the Great Migration and the effect of World War Two. Look back in your book to find information to develop those points.

For more advice check the plan at the end of the book.

11 SEPARATE BUT UNEQUAL

In this chapter you will find out:
- that the Civil Rights movement of the 1950s grew out of discontent at the end of World War Two
- segregation and Jim Crow laws were the first targets of the Civil Rights movement
- a Supreme Court decision in 1954 declared the idea of separate but equal to be unlawful
- when Black students went to school they had to be protected by US soldiers
- the issue of school desegregation became a struggle between state law and federal law.

When Black American soldiers returned from World War Two they found racism still existed at home. They wanted a change. They wanted Civil Rights. They said, 'No more Jim Crow'.

SOURCE 11.1

I think people became more aware that something had to be done about the fact that Black soldiers were fighting overseas for their country and when they came home they would be coming back to a situation that said, 'You're a second class citizen.' I think that's what started the Civil Rights movement of the 1950s and 1960s.

The movement of Black people to the north made all of America aware of 'the race problem'. Segregation and discrimination were no longer seen as problems which only existed in the South. The first aim of the Civil Rights movement in the 1950s was to get rid of segregation and the Jim Crow Laws.

CIVIL RIGHTS AND SCHOOLS

One of the first 'sparks' that lit up the Civil Rights movement in the 1950s was an argument in a town called Topeka in the state of Kansas. The argument was about which school an eight year old girl called Linda Brown should go to. Linda Brown's father thought it was wrong that his daughter should go to a school for Black children that was further away from her home and was less well looked after than nearby schools for White children.

'BROWN V THE TOPEKA BOARD OF EDUCATION'

With the help of the NAACP Linda Brown's father took the Topeka School Board to court. The court case was called 'Brown versus the Topeka Board of Education' and eventually reached the Supreme Court.

You should remember that in 1896 the Supreme Court had decided that segregation was acceptable. The Supreme Court said that Black people and White people should have 'separate but equal' facilities, which included schools.

On Monday, May 17, 1954 the Supreme Court completely changed the decision reached nearly 60 years earlier.

The Court declared that 'separate education facilities are inherently unequal'. In other words the Supreme Court said the idea of 'separate but equal' had no place in modern America. It decided that segregated schools were unequal and that schools should be *desegregated* . The Supreme Court also argued that separating children in the schools because of the colour of their skin:

SOURCE 11.2

… causes a feeling of inferiority as to their status in the community that may affect their hearts and minds in a way unlikely ever to be undone.

The Court's decision was very important for the Civil Rights movement of the 1950s.

The case of Brown v the Topeka Board of Education and the Supreme Court decision was the first victory for Civil Rights campaigners. The problem now was how to make southern states desegregate their schools. By the end of 1956 not one Black child attended a White school in the South. Most southern states believed the Supreme Court was out of touch with the realities of Southern life.

Not everybody was happy with the decision of the Supreme Court. A Southern judge said:

SOURCE 11.3

Black Monday is the name used to describe Monday, May 17, 1954. Black for darkness and terror. Black meaning the absence of light and wisdom.

Even the President of the USA, when he heard about the decision of the Supreme Court, said:

SOURCE 11.4

I don't believe you can change the hearts of men with a law.

LITTLE ROCK, ARKANSAS, 1957

Southern states tried to ignore the Supreme Court's decision. Schools in the South which did try to desegregate were met by furious White racist mobs. The mobs, along with Ku Klux Klan members, attacked Black students. Schools were even blown up. The most famous struggle to integrate schools was in Little Rock, the capital city of Arkansas. The Central High School decided that it would take in nine Black students on September 3, 1957.

The governor of Arkansas, who was called Orval Faubus, was against integration. He sent state soldiers to surround the school and they did not let Black children in the school. An angry mob of White protesters who did not believe in school integration also surrounded the school.

SOURCE 11.5 *Elizabeth Eckford had to face an angry White mob in her way to Central High School, Little Rock*

The first Black student who tried to get in to Central High School was called Elizabeth Eckford.

The photograph shows her trying to get to school.

This is how Elizabeth Eckford remembers her attempts to get to school:

SOURCE 11.6 Elizabeth Eckford (aged 15)

My knees stared to shake and I wondered if I would make it to school. The crowd moved closer and closer. Somebody started yelling 'Drag her over to this tree! Let's take care of that nigger.'

SOURCE 11.7 *US troops were used to protect black children going to school in Little Rock, Arkansas*

The President of the USA was no longer willing to have individual states in the USA ignoring federal law so he ordered the Governor of Arkansas to remove the state soldiers. The President even sent 1000 US soldiers to protect the Black children on their way to school.

The soldiers stayed in Little Rock for a year and they even patrolled the school corridors to make sure the children were safe. Naturally the events in Little Rock, Arkansas attracted worldwide attention to the Civil Rights movement.

JAMES MEREDITH AND MISSISSIPPI LAW SCHOOL

Despite the 1954 Supreme Court decision making segregated schools illegal, other Southern states tried to oppose the decision. In 1962 a Black student, James Meredith, attempted to attend the University of Mississippi law school. His admission was blocked, and during the violence that followed, federal troops were once again used to restore order and enforce national law.

SOURCE 11.8 *James Meredith also had to be protected by US troops – just to attend university!*

The Mississippi authorities tried to ban him from university because he was Black. However the Federal government decided that Meredith should be allowed into the law school. On Sunday, September 30, 1962, 123 federal marshals, 316 US border patrolmen, and 97 federal prison guards escorted Meredith onto the college campus. Facing Meredith and his protectors was a mob of over 2,000 men and women. Riots broke out and two journalists were killed.

President Kennedy had to send in *sixteen thousand* troops to protect Meredith and restore order at the university. Twenty-eight US marshals had been shot and another 160 of the law enforcers were injured. Federal troops remained at the university for over a year to protect one Black student.

WHAT DO YOU THINK?

Was the President of the USA justified in using so many troops and law enforcement officers to protect only one Black student?

Chapter summary
- The Supreme Court decided in 1954 that the idea of 'separate but equal' was illegal.
- The Supreme Court decided that segregated schools were illegal.
- Many states in the South did not want to desegregate their schools.
- US soldiers were used to protect Black students when they went to school.

QUESTION PRACTICE

Look carefully at the photographs and drawings in this chapter.

1 Are the pictures in this chapter equally useful as historical evidence?

Outcome 3

SOURCE A was written by a young Black soldier when he heard about the Supreme Court's decision in 1954.

On Monday, May 17, 1954 I felt that at last the government was willing to assert itself, even for Negroes. I was sure this was the beginning of a new era in American Democracy.

2 Why was the Black soldier so excited about the Court's decision?

Outcome 2

QUESTION PRACTICE

3 Explain how the Supreme Court decision of 1954 was very different from the Supreme Court's decision in 1896.

Outcome 2

SOURCE B is from an interview with Elizabeth Eckford.

I sat down and the mob crowded round. Just then a White man sat down beside me. He raised my chin and said, 'Don't let them see you cry.' Then a White lady – she was very nice – put me on the bus and sat next to me.

Compare Source B with the photograph of Elizabeth Eckford going to school in Little Rock (Source 11.5).

4 Does the photograph give an accurate impression of Elizabeth Eckford's first day experiences when she tried to attend Little Rock High School?

THE MONTGOMERY BUS BOYCOTT, 1955

In this chapter you will find out:
◆ why there was a bus boycott in Montgomery, Alabama
◆ why the bus boycott was successful
◆ why the bus boycott had important results for the Civil Rights movement.

SOURCE 12.1 *When Rosa Parks refused to give up her seat on a bus to a White person she sparked the Montgomery Bus Boycott*

ROSA PARKS

In December 1955 a woman called Rosa Parks was returning home from work. She was tired. She got on a bus and sat down. As the bus started to fill up she was asked to stand up to allow another passenger to sit down. She refused and was arrested. A very important stage in the campaign for Civil Rights had started.

The place was Montgomery, Alabama. Rosa Parks was Black. The passenger who wanted to use her seat was White. Segregation laws in Montgomery provided seats on the buses for Black passengers. When there were no seats left and White passengers got on, Black people were expected to stand up and allow the White passengers to sit down.

One year before Rosa's arrest a letter written to the Mayor of Montgomery had outlined the problem:

SOURCE 12.2

75% of the riders on the buses are Negroes. If the Negroes did not use the buses the bus company could not operate. More and more of our people are already arranging with neighbours and friends to keep from being insulted and humiliated by bus drivers. Plans are being made to ride less, or not at all, on our buses.

The mayor of Montgomery refused to stop segregation on buses which meant that Black passengers continued to be 'humiliated'. Black passengers still had to pay their fare at the front door but could only take their seat when they walked to the back door of the bus to get on.

BOYCOTT THE BUSES

Rosa Parks was not just any Black woman. She had been an active member of the NAACP for many years. Her refusal to give up her seat had been planned by local Civil Rights leaders. When she was arrested fifty Black leaders met in a Montgomery church to discuss their plans. They agreed to *boycott* the city bus system. A boycott means that something is avoided or not used. In this case the Black population refused to use the buses in Montgomery, Alabama.

The bus boycott would also gain publicity for the cause of Civil Rights.

The bus boycott soon began to hurt the bus company. Since Black Americans made up 60 to 70% of all bus riders, the bus company was faced with a choice – desegregate its buses or go out of business. For the first time the Black population had shown its economic power.

The boycott, which lasted for more than a year, was very effective. The Black population 'pooled' or shared their cars. The police in Montgomery tried to stop them car sharing. In a later interview Rosa Parks described how she was arrested twice – the first time for riding on a bus, the second time, when she was car sharing, was for not riding on a bus!

MARTIN LUTHER KING

Throughout the bus boycott, a young Black preacher inspired the Black population of Montgomery to keep up the pressure for their Civil Rights. His name was Martin Luther King and he was to become one of the most famous Black leaders this century.

This extract is from a speech Martin Luther King gave in Montgomery, Alabama at the time of the bus boycott:

SOURCE 12.4

There comes a time when people get tired – tired of being segregated and humiliated: tired of being kicked about by the brutal feet of oppression.

Eventually the courts decided that segregation on Montgomery's buses was against the Constitution of the USA. The buses were officially desegregated in December 1956. However the bus company had started to desegregate anyway. They could not afford to lose Black passengers.

THE EFFECTS OF THE BOYCOTT

In one sense desegregation was a legal victory for Black Americans but in another sense it showed the economic power of Black Americans if they united together.

SOURCE 12.3 *Martin Luther King was only 26 when he helped organise and lead the bus boycott*

On its own the bus boycott only had limited success. It did not end all segregation. Montgomery was still a segregated town. There were still White only theatres, pool rooms and restaurants.

However, the bus boycott had shown Black Americans in the South what could be achieved by organised protest. Peaceful, non-violent protest had won a victory. Martin Luther King, along with the Reverend Ralph Abernathy who helped organise the boycott, became the leaders of the new Civil Rights movement.

THE CREATION OF THE SCLC

Shortly after the boycott Martin Luther King, Ralph Abernathy and other church men formed an organisation called the Southern Christian Leadership Conference (SCLC) to campaign for Civil Rights. It started in 1957. The SCLC supported Martin Luther King's ideas about peaceful, non-violent protest.

Later you will find out that the SCLC was involved in many of the most famous protests of the early 1960s. Martin Luther King was elected president of the SCLC.

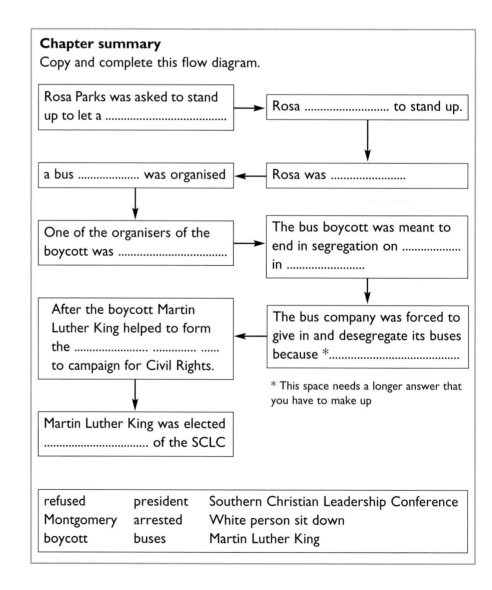

Chapter summary
Copy and complete this flow diagram.

| Rosa Parks was asked to stand up to let a .... | → | Rosa .... to stand up. |

| a bus .... was organised | ← | Rosa was .... |

| One of the organisers of the boycott was .... | → | The bus boycott was meant to end in segregation on .... in .... |

| After the boycott Martin Luther King helped to form the .... to campaign for Civil Rights. | ← | The bus company was forced to give in and desegregate its buses because *................ |

* This space needs a longer answer that you have to make up

| Martin Luther King was elected .... of the SCLC |

refused	president	Southern Christian Leadership Conference
Montgomery	arrested	White person sit down
boycott	buses	Martin Luther King

QUESTION PRACTICE

SOURCE A From a speech by Martin Luther King on December 5, 1955

We are here because of the bus situation in Montgomery. We are here because we are determined to get the situation corrected.

1 Describe the main events of the Montgomery bus boycott.

Outcome 1

SOURCE B (From the same speech)

On so many occasions Negroes have been intimidated and humiliated and oppressed because of the sheer fact they are Negroes. The only weapon we have is the weapon of non violent protest ... The great glory of American democracy is the right to protest for right.

2 Why is source B useful as evidence of Martin Luther King's views about protest?

Outcome 3

QUESTION PRACTICE

This question is to be answered as an 8 mark essay.

SOURCE C is from a book called *The Eyes on the Prize*, published in 1991

By the beginning of the following year, after a long, hard and dangerous struggle, it was clear that the events that transpired (happened) in Montgomery marked a mass based new beginning.

3 Do you agree that the Montgomery bus boycott marked a 'mass based new beginning'?

Outcome 1

For more advice about how to write this answer look at page 120 at the end of this book.

In this chapter you will find out:
- how Martin Luther King became an important leader of the Civil Rights Movement
- why Martin Luther King believed in non-violent protest
- what is meant by non-violent civil disobedience.

Under the leadership of Martin Luther King the Civil Rights campaign in the late 1950s and early 1960s used non-violent, peaceful protest.

Non-violent Protest
1950s until middle 1960s

No segregation in this nation

No more Jim Crow

We shall overcome

Main leader: Martin Luther King

WHO WAS MARTIN LUTHER KING?

Martin Luther King Jnr., was born on Jan. 15, 1929, in Atlanta, Georgia. His father was a church minister who also was called Martin. That is why Martin Luther King often has Jnr for Junior after his name. When he was a boy growing up in Atlanta, Martin Luther King experienced segregation and discrimination for himself.

In 1953 Martin Luther King married Coretta Scott and in 1954, King was given his first job as pastor at the Dexter Avenue Baptist Church in Montgomery, Alabama. He was still only 25 years old.

SOURCE 13.1 *Martin Luther King and his wife Coretta Scott King*

Martin Luther King became a Baptist minister. Throughout his life he used his ability as a preacher to speak up for the poor, the disadvantaged and Black Americans across the USA. In the 1950s and 1960s Martin Luther King's main target was segregation and discrimination against Black Americans.

HOW DID MARTIN LUTHER KING BECOME FAMOUS?

Martin Luther King and his wife, Coretta, were in Montgomery for less than a year when the bus boycott began. King's successful organisation of the year-long Montgomery bus boycott, with the help of another church minister called Ralph Abernathy, made Martin Luther King into a well known national leader of the Civil Rights movement. After the bus boycott success, Martin Luther King travelled all over the South making speeches and encouraging Black Americans to stand up for their rights. In 1958 he wrote his first book which was called *Stride Toward Freedom*.

In 1960 Martin Luther King became president of the Southern Christian Leadership Conference (SCLC). In the early 1960s Martin Luther King led many demonstrations in the South which aimed at ending segregation and allowing Black Americans to vote freely. In 1964 Martin Luther King became world famous when he made a speech which became known as the 'I Have a Dream' speech and Time magazine (a very important national magazine in the USA) chose Martin Luther King as their Man of the Year; this was the first time a Black American had ever won the title. Later in 1964 Martin Luther King also won the Nobel Peace Prize. He was the youngest man ever to win it. He was still only 35 years old.

WHAT DID MARTIN LUTHER KING BELIEVE IN?

King had studied the tactics of a man called Mahatma Gandhi who had used non-violent protest successfully against the British rulers of India in the 1940s. Gandhi believed the best way to protest against a system that used force to maintain its power was by non-violent civil disobedience. Martin Luther King, when speaking to bus boycotters in Montgomery, Alabama, made it clear that he would not use violence. He said:

SOURCE 13.2 Martin Luther King in December 1955

In our protest there will be no cross burnings. No White person will be taken from his house by a hooded Negro mob and brutally murdered. There will be no threats or bullying. Love your enemies and pray for them.

Martin Luther King also believed that civil disobedience was the way to gain Civil Rights in America. King believed if a law was wrong then the citizens of the country had the right and the responsibility to protest about it. If he and his followers were arrested that was fine – because the jails all across the South would be filled with Civil Rights protesters and that would give the campaign even more publicity. When Martin Luther King spoke to a crowd of White racists outside a church in Alabama, he said he would not obey evil laws. He also said that he and his followers intended to wear down the resistance of White racists by using endless protests.

When Martin Luther King became president of the Southern Christian Leadership Conference (SCLC) in 1960 he became more and more involved in the use of non violent civil disobedience as a way of campaigning for Civil Rights in the early 1960s.

In the next chapter you will find out what happened to Martin Luther King and his followers as they tried to use his non violent civil disobedience tactics to fight segregation and discrimination in the South through the late 1950s and early 1960s. You will then find out more about his later work and also how he died.

FACTFILE

What was the Southern Christian Leadership Conference (SCLC)?

The Southern Christian Leadership Conference (SCLC) was founded in 1957. It was organised by Martin Luther King, Ralph Abernathy and other Civil Rights leaders. The SCLC supported King's ideas about non-violent protest. In the early 1960s the SCLC campaigned for desegregation in the South

---

Chapter summary

◆ Martin Luther King became one of the most important Civil Rights leaders.

◆ Martin Luther King believed in using non-violent protest.

◆ Martin Luther King believed that laws which were unfair should be disobeyed.

◆ Many students supported the ideas of Martin Luther King.

◆ The Southern Christian Leadership Conference was led by Martin Luther King.

◆ The Southern Christian Leadership Conference was an important protest organisation in the early 1960s.

QUESTION PRACTICE

SOURCE A is from a speech by Martin Luther King in 1955.

There comes a time when people get tired ... We are tired of being segregated and humiliated, tired of being kicked about. We have no choice but to protest.

1 Describe the ways in which Martin Luther King intended to protest.

Outcome 1

SOURCE B was written by Martin Luther King in a book called *Stride Toward Freedom*.

It was January 30, 1956. After putting the baby to bed, Coretta went to the living room to look at television. About nine thirty she heard a noise like someone had thrown a brick. In a matter of seconds an explosion rocked the house. A bomb had gone off in our porch.

2 Why do you think Martin Luther King's house was attacked?

Outcome 2

QUESTION PRACTICE

SOURCE C is from a speech given by Martin Luther King in 1955.

In our protest there will be no cross burnings. No White person will be taken from his house by a hooded Negro mob and brutally murdered. There will be no threats or bullying. Love your enemies and pray for them.

SOURCE D is from another Black leader called Malcolm X speaking in 1965.

I don't go along with any kind of non-violence unless everybody's going to be non-violent. If they make the Ku Klux Klan non-violent I'll be non-violent. You get freedom by letting your enemy know that you'll ... fight them, and then you'll get your freedom.

3 Compare Sources C and D as evidence of differences of opinion about the best way to achieve Civil Rights.

Outcome 3

14   SIT INS

In this chapter you will find out:
- that by 1960 little progress had been made towards full Civil Rights
- that new organisations grew up with new ideas about protests
- how sit ins and freedom rides gained national publicity for the Civil Rights Movement.

THE CIVIL RIGHTS ACT OF 1957

After the events in Montgomery, Alabama and Little Rock, Arkansas, the US government introduced the Civil Rights Act in 1957. The President at the time was called Dwight Eisenhower and he was not convinced that a Civil Rights law would work. He said:

SOURCE 14.1

I personally believe if you try to go too far and involve the emotions of so many millions of Americans, you're making a mistake.

Nevertheless, the act passed, due to the efforts of a politician called Lyndon B. Johnson.

The Civil Rights Act of 1957

1 A national Civil Rights Commission was started.
2 The Federal Justice Department would support Black Americans if they went to court because they could not vote freely.

The Civil Rights Act of 1957 was not a huge step, but it was the first national Civil Rights Act for nearly 100 years.

Opinion was divided as to the importance of the Civil Rights Act. On one hand it seemed to show that the Federal government was no longer willing to allow the southern states to do as they pleased as far as race relations were concerned. On the other hand some Civil Rights campaigners were disappointed with the limited power of the Act. By 1959 the new Civil Rights Act had not added a single southern Black vote to the voting register. The problem of voter registration was one that Martin Luther King started to tackle in 1964 and 1965. You will find out more about that later.

PRESSURE FOR MORE CHANGE

The pressure for Civil Rights continued to grow during the early 1960s. The years 1960 and 1961 were a time of big change in the Civil Rights movement. Although the Supreme Court's decision of

1954 had outlawed school segregation there had been very few moves in the South to end discrimination and segregation.

SHOULD PROTEST BE VIOLENT OR NON-VIOLENT?

By 1960 many Black Americans were tired of waiting for change. In 1959 some Black Americans even demanded the right to use armed self-defence against White persecution.

SOURCE 14.2 Robert F Williams, Liberation magazine

I believe Negroes must be willing to defend themselves, their women, their children and their homes. Negroes must protect themselves. It is obvious the Federal government will not put an end to lynching; therefore it becomes necessary for us to stop lynching with violence.

In 1960 a new, younger and more instant form of protest was born. The actions of Black and White students put new life into the Civil Rights movement. Old organisations had to rethink their protest methods. New protest organisations were born. National publicity for the new protest methods created mass support for the Civil Rights movement among all sections of the Black American population. Above all, the new protesters believed in the non-violent methods of Martin Luther King.

Four events in the early 1960s eventually forced the President, John F. Kennedy, and the US government to pass a new Civil Rights law.

These four events were:
- the sit-in campaigns
- the freedom rides
- the protests in Birmingham, Alabama
- The March on Washington

THE SIT IN CAMPAIGN

Despite protests, Supreme Court decisions and the new Civil Rights Act, segregation was still very common in the Southern states.

On 1 February, 1960, four students ordered sodas, coffee, and doughnuts but their order was refused. The students were sitting at a Whites-only lunch counter in Greensboro. Greensboro is in the state of North Carolina.

In Greensboro, Black people had to stay out of White-owned restaurants, to use Black only drinking fountains and restrooms and to sit in the rear of Greensboro city buses. The Greensboro Four, as they were later called, were attacking segregation in Greensboro.

When the four Black students sat down at the 'Whites only' counter they faced a sign attached to the wall:

Lunch counter
No Niggers Served Here

The Greensboro Four were Franklin McCain, Joseph McNeil, Ezell Blair Jr. and David Richmond. In 1960 they were still teenagers and McCain later said he expected to be arrested, beaten to a pulp or worse.

The students were told to move but they refused. Next day they returned with 80 more Black and White protesters. The students 'sat in' all day despite insults and attacks.

SOURCE 14.3 *Black and White students were physically and verbally abused when they sat at a 'Whites Only' lunch counter.*

The students were followers of Martin Luther King's ideas about non-violent protest. Quickly the idea of sit-in protests spread across the South. By the end of 1960, 70 000 protesters had taken part in sit ins.

Non-violent protest was met by White violence. Night after night TV viewers across America saw peaceful students being insulted, beaten and dragged off to jail. Television became an important weapon for Civil Rights campaigners. Night after night TV news showed non-violent protesters being beaten up, attacked by dogs or worse – just because they wanted Civil Rights.

A new slogan was heard from Black protesters:

Fill the Jails!

Martin Luther King taught that civil disobedience was a valuable weapon. If jails were filled with protesters the daily business of law courts would be disrupted. As one young student protester said:

SOURCE 14.4

We are willing to go to jail, be spat upon and even suffer physical violence to obtain First Class Citizenship.

Jails in police stations across the South reached bursting point. Something would have to be done. Restaurants and cafes across the south could not afford the bad publicity and loss of business. The result was that by the summer of 1960 there were almost no more segregated lunch counters in the South. Non-violent protest, national TV coverage and the need to avoid bad publicity had forced restaurants and cafes to desegregate.

HOW SUCCESSFUL WERE THE SIT INS?

There are different opinions about the effectiveness of the sit-in campaign.
- Some Civil Rights workers believed that the sit-ins showed students that they could take action themselves. Young Black people realised that they could make a difference to Civil Rights. The sit-ins also became national news and that forced many Whites to take notice of the 'race issue'.
- A different point of view is that sit-ins only achieved limited success in some of the towns and cities where the protests were used.
- Much more needed to be done.
  Everyone knew that sit-ins would not win full Civil Rights across America but they were important. Sit-ins showed ordinary Black Americans that their actions could make a difference. Ella J. Baker, a Civil Rights campaigner summed up the feelings that sit-ins were only the first step towards bigger changes.

SOURCE 14.5

Sit-ins and other demonstrations are concerned with something much bigger than a hamburger or a giant sized Coke. Negro and White students, North and South, are seeking to rid America of racial segregation and discrimination, not only at lunch counters but in every aspect of life.

Chapter summary
- Sit-ins began in Greensboro, North Carolina in 1960.
- Sit-ins were an example of non-violent civil disobedience.
- The purpose of the early sit-ins was to end segregation at lunch counters.
- Sit-ins were only part of a bigger protest campaign against segregation and discrimination in the South.

QUESTION PRACTICE

SOURCE A is from an interview with Franklin McCain, one of the 'Greensboro Four' sit-in students.

... I think it was Joseph who said, 'Let's just go down and ask for service. We'll stay until we get served.' We never expected to be served.

1 What was so special about Franklin McCain and his friends going for lunch?

Outcome 1

2 Why was the sit-in campaign so important to the Civil Rights Movement?

Outcome 2

QUESTION PRACTICE

SOURCE B is also from an interview with Franklin McCain, one of the 'Greensboro Four' sit-in students.

The individual who had most influence on us was Gandhi, more than anyone else. During the bus boycott we were just kids and we barely heard of Martin Luther King ... yes Martin Luther King was a hero, no he was not the individual that we had upmost in our mind when we started the sit-in movement.

3 Why did McCain credit Gandhi more than King as the most important influence in the sit-in campaign?

Outcome 2

15

THE FREEDOM RIDES

In this chapter you will find out:
◆ why freedom rides happened
◆ how freedom rides showed that racism still existed in the South
◆ why the freedom rides became a struggle between Federal and State authority
◆ how freedom rides gained national publicity for the Civil Rights Movement.

In 1960 a Supreme Court decision had banned segregation in public areas such as rest rooms, waiting rooms and restaurants for travellers using buses that went from one state to another.

In 1961 a group of Black and White members of an a non-violent protest group called CORE – the Congress of Racial Equality – wanted to see if such segregation really had ended.

This is what one White student called William Mahoney found at the first stopping point on his journey:

SOURCE 15.1

'At our first stop in Virginia I saw what a Southern White called separate but equal. A modern rest station with gleaming counters was labelled 'White' and a small wooden shack beside it was tagged 'Colored'. The colored waiting room was filthy and in need of repair and overcrowded.'

FACTFILE

What was CORE?

The Congress of Racial Equality (CORE) was founded in 1942. Its aim was to fight discrimination against Black people by using non-violent, direct action. Both White and Black people were members of CORE. In the early 1960s CORE organised the Freedom Rides.

In the mid-1960s CORE changed its ideas. It supported new, more extreme ideas such as Black Nationalism. CORE demanded the right for Black communities to be self governing where Black Americans were in a majority.

The intention of CORE was to gain publicity for their protest. They also believed in non-violent protest. So they began the 'Freedom Rides', adding to the pressure on the government to do something to improve Civil Rights in the early 1960s.

WHAT WAS A FREEDOM RIDE?

In May 1961 13 members of the Congress of Racial Equality rode from Washington to New Orleans in the southern state of Mississippi. The plan was that Black students would try to use 'Whites only' wash rooms at stopping points along the route. The students became known as 'Freedom Riders' and the bus journeys were called 'Freedom Rides'.

RACIST VIOLENCE

The Freedom Riders were met with heavy resistance from Southern Whites who knew the route which the students were following. When the buses arrived in Alabama, the Klan was waiting for them. In Anniston, Alabama, the two 'Freedom' buses were stopped and burned. Passengers who tried to get off were beaten. The students then travelled to Birmingham, Alabama where they got on another interstate bus. The bus was again stopped and eight White men boarded the bus. They brutally beat the students with sticks and chains. One of the students, James Peck, had to have fifty stitches in his head.

SOURCE 15.2 *Buses carrying Freedom Riders were attacked and set on fire*

Even when faced by such vicious attacks the students stuck to their non-violent protest beliefs.

Student William Mahoney was arrested and given two weeks in prison. Mahoney described his time in prison:

SOURCE 15.3

Morale remained high. Insults and brutality became the subject of jokes. The jailers' hostility was broken down by responding to it with respect and good humour.

Martin Luther King was horrified by the actions of the White bullies but he was more worried about the safety of the students. He tried to get the students to stop.

FEDERAL ACTION

Even President Kennedy was concerned about the 'Freedom Rides' and he sent one of his advisors to see first hand what was happening. When the President's advisor arrived, he was beaten unconscious.

The Freedom Rides drew national attention, especially from middle-class Northerners who were shocked by what they saw on television. Eventually police escorts were provided for the riders, although this did not prevent further violence.

The FBI was then sent in to investigate the violence against the students and US law officers were also sent in to protect the students. As the risk of serious violence increased Martin Luther

FACTFILE

Student Non-violent Coordinating Committee (SNCC) – Part I

The Student Nonviolent Coordinating Committee (SNCC) was founded in the United States in 1960, with the help of Dr. Martin Luther King, to work for Civil Rights in the deep South. It was also called 'Snick'.

The movement grew out of a sit-in at Greensboro, North Carolina. In addition to coordinating sit-ins in the South, SNCC organised voter-registration campaigns.

Chapter Summary
- Freedom Rides were organised by CORE.
- CORE stood for the Congress of Racial Equality.
- The aim of the Freedom Riders was to get rid of segregation on interstate buses.
- When Freedom Riders went into the South they were attacked by White mobs.
- TV pictures of White violence shocked the USA.
- The Federal Government was forced to protect the Freedom Riders.
- The Federal Government ordered segregation to end in all public transport.
- Freedom Rides were another example of a successful non-violent protest.

King once again attempted to get the students to stop, but they refused. Both CORE and another student group – the Students Non-violent Coordinating Committee (SNCC) – agreed to continue the bus rides.

Eventually, in the face of national publicity and pressure to change, new orders were sent to all interstate bus companies that ended segregation at interstate bus stations.

Finally, in late 1961, the US government ordered the end of segregation in airports, rail and bus stations.

HOW IMPORTANT WERE THE FREEDOM RIDES?

There are different opinions about how important the freedom rides were. Some historians think they were very important. A CORE publicity leaflet said:

SOURCE 15.4

The freedom rides, like the sit-ins before them, demonstrated that anyone who opposed segregation ... could drive a nail into the coffin of Jim Crow. They helped the spread of Civil Rights through the south.

Many people agree that of all the tactics used by the Civil Rights Movement, the Freedom Riders did the most to increase support for the Civil Rights movement.

The Freedom Riders, like the sit-ins before them, were successful in making northern White Americans more and more sympathetic towards the Civil Rights cause.

Attacks by the Klan and fire-bombed buses were pictured in national newspapers and on television. The situation in the South could not be ignored by Federal government for much longer.

On the other hand, there is a view that the Freedom Rides did little to change the real problem which was that Black Americans had little power themselves to change the way the country was run. As James M. Lawson, writing in the Southern Patriot newspaper reported in 1961:

SOURCE 15.5

The Freedom Rides won concessions but not real changes. Police help keep the peace and let us use interstate rest rooms but there will be no revolution until we see Negro faces in powerful positions in this country.

QUESTION PRACTICE

SOURCE A is from a recent book about the Civil Rights Movement.

The freedom riders were successful in publicising the way Black people were treated in the southern states. Public opinion polls showed Americans increasingly sympathetic to the Civil Rights cause.

1 What did the freedom riders hope to achieve?

Outcome 2

SOURCE B was written by James M. Lawson Jr. in 1961. He believed a non-violent campaign would start a total revolution that would change society.

Let us prepare for mass non-violent action in the Deep South. Let us recruit people who would be willing to stay in jail indefinitely. The Freedom Rides were a start of this.

2 How useful is Source B for finding out about the non-violent campaign for Civil Rights?

QUESTION PRACTICE

Extended answer

Question:
The sit ins and Freedom Rides achieved a lot for the Civil Rights Movement. Do you agree?   *Outcome 1*

You must show that you understand what the sit ins were and what they tried to achieve.

You must show that you understand what the freedom rides were and what they tried to achieve.

Look at the evidence that supports the view that they did a lot for the Civil Rights movement and balance your answer with evidence that they did not do a great deal for the movement.

For more help in planning this answer look at the advice at the end of this book.

16

BIRMINGHAM, ALABAMA 1963

In this chapter you will find out:
◆ why a large Civil Rights demonstration was planned in Birmingham, Alabama
◆ why America was shocked by the Birmingham demonstration
◆ why the demonstration can be seen as a turning point in the Civil Rights movement.

In January 1963, Martin Luther King announced that SCLC was going to Birmingham, Alabama to try to stop segregation there.

George Wallace was the new governor of Alabama and was against Civil Rights. He said:

SOURCE 16.1

Segregation now, segregation tomorrow, segregation forever.

In April and May 1963 a new protest campaign was launched in Birmingham, Alabama.

WHY WAS BIRMINGHAM CHOSEN FOR THE DEMONSTRATION?

Martin Luther King supplied the answer.

SOURCE 16.2

I think I should give the reason for my being in Birmingham. Birmingham is probably the most segregated city in the United States. Its ugly record of police brutality is known in every section of the country. Its unjust treatment of Negroes in the courts is a notorious reality. There have been more unsolved bombings of Negro homes and churches in Birmingham than in any city in this nation. These are the hard, brutal and unbelievable facts.

Martin Luther King knew that Civil Rights protesters would be risking their lives when they arrived in Birmingham. The Klan in Birmingham was one of the most violent in the entire country. They were responsible for dozens of bombings throughout the area. One of the Civil Rights leaders called Birmingham 'Bombingham' because of the violence that was common in the area. It was also no secret that the Klan had the support of the Birmingham police department, led by Eugene 'Bull' Connor.

However the Civil Rights leaders knew that if they could lead a successful demonstration in Birmingham then they might spark off big changes across the South. As Martin Luther King said:

SOURCE 16.3

The campaign in Birmingham will surely be the toughest fight of our Civil Rights career. It could successfully break the back of segregation all over our nation.

The two main leaders of the demonstration in Birmingham were Martin Luther King and the Reverend Fred Shuttlesworth. They had made clear their objectives – to desegregate public facilities and department stores. However even those limited aims were too much for the Birmingham police.

Even before the march started, King and Shuttlesworth were arrested for planning to break an order not to march.

THE LETTER FROM BIRMINGHAM JAIL

Even local church men thought that the Civil Rights campaigners were asking for too much and that they should be patient and wait for more gradual changes in American society. While he was in prison Martin Luther King wrote his famous reply to those who said that Black Americans should wait for White America to give slow changes.

SOURCE 16.4

I guess it is easy for those who have never felt segregation to say wait. But when you have seen vicious mobs lynch your fathers and mothers and drown your brothers and sisters ... when you have seen the majority of your 20 million Negro brothers smothering in an airtight cage of poverty ... when your tongue becomes twisted as you try to explain to your six year old daughter why she can't go to the amusement park advertised on TV and see the tears welling up in her little eyes when you tell her that Funtown is closed to colored children ... then you will know why it is difficult to wait.

THE DEMONSTRATION BEGINS

On April 20 King and Shuttlesworth were released from prison and the marchers were ready to begin. A plan was made which would use school children to lead the march. The SCLC knew the importance of publicity. TV footage of school children being arrested would embarrass the city and gain sympathy for the Civil Rights movement.

On May 2 the march began – and Bull Connor was waiting for them. Connor was a racist and he was determined not to give in to the Civil Rights demonstrators. As soon as they began to march, he ordered the arrest of all of the students. Over nine hundred children from the age of 6 to 18 were jailed.

The following day, Connor called out the water cannons and the dogs. As marchers came parading down the streets, the police attacked. Bull Connor used fire hoses, billy clubs (like baseball bats) and dogs to attack the peaceful protesters. America watched in horror as school-age children were savagely beaten and bitten. This is what some of the protesters said:

> I was only nine years old. I was in jail for seven days.

> The water was very strong. I got wet and I was nearly bitten.

> The police thought it was funny to let the dogs jump at us.

SOURCE 16.5

SOURCE 16.6 *Non-violent protesters were attacked by police with dogs*

The whole nation was outraged. A well known singer songwriter at that time was Phil Ochs. This is what he wrote in a song called 'Talking Birmingham Jam':

SOURCE 16.7 *Talking Birmingham Jam* by Phil Ochs

Well, all the signs said Welcome in,
Welcome if you're White my friend.
Come along and watch the fights
While we feed our dogs on Civil Rights.

Well I've seen travel in many ways
I've travelled in cars and old subways
But in Birmingham some people chose
To fly down the street from a fire hose.

Well I said there must be some men around
There can't be only you dogs in town
They said 'Sure we have old Bull Connor
There he goes, walkin' yonder'

So, I asked em' how they spend their time
With segregation on their mind.
They said if you don't like to live this way
Get outta here, go back to the USA

The next day, things were different. As the marchers came down the street, Connor again ordered his men to attack. Instead, firemen refused to turn on their hoses and many of the police would not attack the marchers again. However several hundred protesters were still arrested that day.

A DEAL IS MADE

By the fourth day of demonstrations both sides in 'the battle of Birmingham' were having second thoughts. Martin Luther King wanted to call the march off. He was concerned about the violence being suffered by the demonstrators. They were getting 'good' publicity but at a terrible cost. However it was decided to continue the marches.

If you had been the leader of the Civil Right demonstrations, would you have stopped the demonstrations? Remember that you cannot use the benefit of hindsight. In other words you have no idea what will happen next. You don't know that the march will be a success. You only know that your young protesters are being hurt.

On the other side of the 'battle', local business men were desperate for a solution. Their trade had collapsed and the bad publicity that Birmingham was getting on national TV was likely to damage their businesses for a long time. The businessmen offered a deal. They agreed that rest rooms, lunch counters, fitting rooms, and drinking fountains would be desegregated within ninety days.

KLAN VIOLENCE

When word leaked out about the deal the local Klan were furious. They rioted in the city and fire-bombed several Black churches, businesses, and homes.

An event in a local motel showed just how closely linked the Klan was to the local law officers. Many of the protesters were staying at the Gaston Motel which was fire-bombed by the Klan. As the occupants ran out of the building, state troopers, ordered to the scene by Governor Wallace and led by Colonel Al Lingo, attacked them. Several of the protesters were seriously injured, but this time they fought back. A riot broke out. When it was all over, forty people had been injured and seven stores were destroyed by fire.

WAS THE BIRMINGHAM DEMONSTRATION A SUCCESS?

It's very likely that Martin Luther King chose to launch a protest campaign in Birmingham because he guessed that Bull Connor would use violence. TV pictures of non-violent protesters being attacked by Alabama police would increase public sympathy and support for the Civil Rights movement across the USA. He was right.

SOURCE 16.8 *TV news shocked America with pictures of water cannons being used against children*

Chapter Summary
- Birmingham, Alabama was the scene of a large Civil Rights demonstration in 1963.
- Martin Luther King claimed that Birmingham was one of the most segregated cities in the USA.
- The demonstrators faced extreme police violence.
- The USA was shocked by TV news coverage of the demonstration.
- The US President ordered Birmingham to stop segregation.
- Some historians say Birmingham was a success because it gained public support for the cause of Civil Rights.
- Some historians say Birmingham was not a total success.

- The world had been shocked by pictures of young children being attacked by police dogs and washed down streets by fire hoses in Birmingham.
- All across America the public wanted change and a week after the attack by Bull Connor's police the Civil Rights demonstrators seemed to have won.
- Public sympathy for Civil Rights was high and the US President, John F. Kennedy, could not ignore the mood of the public. Kennedy ordered an end to segregation in Birmingham.
- Federal authority once again was prepared to force state governments to obey federal laws.

However, this sympathy was gained at a cost:
- The Birmingham campaign was very costly in human life and it damaged support for Martin Luther King.
- Volunteers from all over the North had rushed to Birmingham to help the demonstrators. Many of them were beaten by the police or the Klan.
- Three students from the North were murdered in Mississippi.
- Mississippi NAACP leader Medgar Evers was also murdered in front of his house. Many Black Americans were beginning to wonder if the struggle was worth the cost. They also wondered if non-violence was the best policy.
- On a local level, many Black Americans in Birmingham, and other places chosen for 'publicity' demonstrations, were opposed to the tactics used by the Civil Rights workers. When the Civil Rights marchers left town with the national TV cameras, they had to live with the hostility from Whites.

QUESTION PRACTICE

i1

SOURCE A is part of the agreement reached which ended the Birmingham protest demonstrations in 1963.

Within 30 days 'White only' signs on wash rooms, rest rooms and drinking fountains will be removed. Within 60 days lunch counters will be desegregated.

1 Describe the events in Birmingham in 1963 which led to the promises listed in Source A.   *Outcome 1*

SOURCE B is part of Martin Luther King's letter from Birmingham jail, written in April, 1963.

You may well ask, 'Why direct action? Why sit ins and marches? Isn't negotiation a better path?' You are exactly right. That is the purpose of direct action ... a community that has refused to negotiate is forced to confront (face) the issue (problem).

2 Why is source B a useful source for finding out about non-violent protest?   *Outcome 3*

QUESTION PRACTICE

i2

After the demonstrations in Birmingham, President Kennedy is supposed to have said, 'the Civil Rights people should thank God for Bull Connor'.

3 What do you think President Kennedy meant?
          Outcome 2

After the Birmingham protests a TV reporter said 'sure, thank God for Bull Connor, but also thank the TV cameras and news reporters.'

4 Compare the comments by Kennedy and the reporter. Which of the statements most accurately explains the success of the Birmingham protests?
          Outcome 3

17

PRESIDENT KENNEDY AND THE CIVIL RIGHTS ACT OF 1964

In this chapter you will find out that:

- the US government felt under pressure to improve Civil Rights
- when President Kennedy was assassinated the Civil Rights Movement thought the plans for a new law would be dropped
- a March on Washington was organised to raise national support for the Civil Rights Bill
- at the march, Martin Luther King made his most famous speech
- violence in Birmingham still continued and showed that racism still existed in the South.

KENNEDY'S PROMISE

The protests of the early 1960s – the sit ins, the Freedom Rides and the Birmingham demonstrations – all increased the pressure on President Kennedy to do something about Civil Rights. On the evening of June 11, 1963, Kennedy spoke on national television to explain what he intended to do and why he intended to do it. He said:

SOURCE 17.1

This nation was founded on the principle that all men are created equal … It ought to be possible for every American to enjoy the privileges of being an American without regard to his race or color. If an American, because of his skin colour, cannot eat lunch in a restaurant open to the public, if he cannot send his children to the best school there is, if he cannot vote for the politicians who represent him, … then who would be content with patience and delay? One hundred years of delay have passed since the slaves were freed. The events at Birmingham have so increased the cries for equality that no nation can choose to ignore them.

I am, therefore, asking the Congress to enact legislation (to pass a law) giving all Americans the right to be served in facilities which are open to the public. I am also asking Congress … to end segregation in public schools. Other features will be requested including greater protection for the right to vote.

All this meant that President Kennedy had been convinced that the government of the USA should make a new Civil Rights Law.

THE MARCH ON WASHINGTON, AUGUST 1963

In the 1940s A. Philip Randolph had suggested a March on Washington in an attempt to force the US government to improve Civil Rights. He had been persuaded not to organise the march by promises that Civil Rights would improve. However 20 years later it looked as if nothing had been achieved. Randolph and other Black leaders felt that is was time for a new March on Washington. As Black leaders organised the march, politicians in Washington were afraid that there would be violence. Kennedy, however, saw it as opportunity to gain support from Black Americans.

SOURCE 17.2 *Martin Luther King and other Civil Rights leaders were at the front of the march on Washington.*

One of the main reasons for the march was to gain publicity for the new Civil Rights bill which seemed to be stuck on its path to become a law. President Kennedy had said he would support it but despite what Kennedy promised, Civil Rights leaders knew it would not be easy to get a new Civil Rights law passed. Politicians, such as Governor Wallace of Alabama, had said they would stop it becoming law.

In the summer of 1963 the time seemed right to carry out a March for Jobs and Freedom. Several Black leaders argued that this was a chance to attack the government by making aggressive, angry speeches. One leader called John Lewis, Chairman of SNCC, wanted to attack Kennedy's proposals, because they did not include voting reform. Other leaders said the speeches should aim at winning White sympathy and support.

On August 28, 1963, almost 250 000 men, women, and children gathered beside the Lincoln Memorial. The site was important since it had been President Lincoln who had freed the slaves one hundred years before.

It was a gigantic meeting but some felt that nothing was gained by the march. However, they missed the point. The march itself was not aimed at gaining anything apart from publicity and it achieved that brilliantly. Four national TV channels carried the event 'live'.

'I HAVE A DREAM'

The speech that Martin Luther King gave to the thousands of marchers – and to a worldwide TV audience – has become one of the most famous speeches of the twentieth century.

SOURCE 17.3 *'I have a dream ...'*

It included the following famous lines:

SOURCE 17.4

… I have a dream that my four little children will one day live in a nation where they will not be judged by the colour of their skin but by the content of their character … I have a dream that even the state of Mississippi will one day be transformed into an oasis of freedom and justice. So let freedom ring out. When we allow freedom to ring from every town and every hamlet, from every state and every city we will be able to speed up that day when all God's children will be able to join hands and sing in the words of the old Negro song 'Free at last! Free at last! Great God Almighty, we are Free at last'.

Martin Luther King's dream was not shared by everyone. Many racists were angry at the support and sympathy for the Civil Rights movement. In Birmingham, Alabama, new racist violence again demonstrated that Civil Rights would not be won through speeches alone.

WHAT WAS THE SIXTEENTH STREET CHURCH BOMBING?

Just two weeks after the Washington march, a bomber threw 15 sticks of dynamite into a church's basement. 250 people were in the church at the time. Four young Black girls were in the changing room of the basement. They were killed by the blast which completely destroyed the building. Another 20 people lay seriously injured.

As the police and firemen arrived, the bomber, who was called Robert Chambliss, was seen standing in the crowd watching the fire. Chambliss was a member of the Ku Klux Klan.

WHAT WERE THE RESULTS OF THE BOMBING?

The bombing of the church was another event which turned many Black Americans against Martin Luther King's non-violent protest methods. They wanted revenge for what had happened. Most of the local people felt that local and state police would do nothing to find the bomber. They also felt that the threat of Black violence would bring in federal law officers and soldiers. Maybe then something would be done to protect the Black community against White violence.

THE POWER OF THE VOTE

At first, the threat of violence was supported by many Black leaders but then a new plan developed. Martin Luther King and other non-violent leaders argued that violence would lose sympathy and support from the general public. The only way to get real change was to get rid of the racists in local and state politics. Black Americans were still in the majority in many southern cities and could put their own leaders in positions of power if they got the opportunity to vote for them.

Use your Vote

The problem was that very few Black Americans registered to vote. The Civil Rights movement now aimed to get more Black Americans voting. That meant they had to be able to do so without fear of violence or threats. It also meant that any unfair blocks to stop Black Americans voting would have to be removed.

WHAT DO YOU THINK?

The bomber of the church, Robert Chambliss, was personally responsible for most of the bombings in the state of Alabama.

Several informants gave the name of Chambliss and all the evidence the FBI needed to convict Chambliss of the crime. However, Chambliss was not prosecuted and convicted of the crime until 1977, fourteen years after the murders. Why did it take so long?

◆ The FBI said that if it had revealed its informants to local law officers, the informants would have probably been murdered.

◆ The Civil Rights movement, on the other hand, believed that the FBI protected Chambliss so that there would be a constant threat to the movement. Chambliss was just the sort of man who might be useful to them. At that time the FBI was suspicious about what Martin Luther King was planning. King was under a full scale investigation. He was followed. His phone calls were recorded. Maybe people like Chambliss would be useful to the FBI if they decided it was necessary to assassinate King. What do you think?

THE ASSASSINATION OF PRESIDENT KENNEDY

King and other leaders of the Civil Rights movement felt that they had a friend in President Kennedy. By 1963, Kennedy seemed to wholeheartedly support the movement. However, in November 1963, Kennedy was assassinated.

The 'March on Washington' had put the Civil Rights movement back in the headlines but when President Kennedy was assassinated it looked like the Civil Rights movement had gained nothing. However, the new president, called Lyndon Johnson, made sure that the Civil Rights Act became law.

THE 1964 CIVIL RIGHTS ACT

Years of protests eventually resulted in the 1964 Civil Rights Act. When the Act was being discussed in the US government all Southern politicians fought against it with all their energy. However it did become law, and was the most important new Civil Rights Law at that time. It did a great deal to get rid of discrimination and segregation.

Civil Rights Act 1964

Discrimination on the basis of race in any or all public places in the US was banned. This included petrol stations, restaurants, hotels, movie theatres, airline terminals, etc. An exception was made for places that served less than five people.

Equal opportunities in the work place: it was now unlawful for a business employing more than 25 people to discriminate on the basis of 'race, national origin, religion, or sex.'

The Justice Department was allowed to take to court any state government that still discriminated against Black people.

Chapter Summary

◆ A march on Washington was organised to win support for a new Civil Rights law.

◆ At the end of the march, Martin Luther King made his 'I have a dream' speech.

◆ In November 1963 President Kennedy was assassinated.

◆ Civil Rights leaders thought that the new President would not support Civil Rights.

◆ The Civil Rights Act of 1964 did make discrimination and segregation illegal.

HOW IMPORTANT WAS THE CIVIL RIGHTS ACT OF 1964?

◆ As far as many politicians were concerned the Civil Rights act had gone as far as the law could to help Black Americans.

◆ As far as many Black Americans were concerned the Civil Rights Act was not the end of the road. The new law did nothing to solve discrimination in housing or give Black people a fair and free vote. The act did not end fear and discrimination. The Klan, often helped by the police, still used terror against any Black person who tried to use the freedoms that the act was supposed to guarantee.

◆ Most people agreed that the Civil Rights Act was a big move towards helping Black Americans achieve full Civil Rights.

QUESTION PRACTICE

SOURCE A is from a TV broadcast made by President Kennedy in June 1963.

The events at Birmingham have increased the cries for equality. It ought to be possible for every American to enjoy the privileges of being American without regard to his race or his colour.

1 Why did President Kennedy want to support a new Civil Rights law?

Outcome 2

SOURCE B was part of a speech to be made by John Lewis at the Lincoln Memorial at the end of the March on Washington.

We cannot support the government's Civil Rights Bill for it is too little too late. There is nothing in the law to protect our people from police brutality. There is nothing in the law to protect our young children and old people from police dogs and fire hoses. This law will not help thousands of Black Citizens who want to vote.

2 For what reasons did some Civil Rights leaders not support the Civil Rights Act of 1964? *Outcome 1*

QUESTION PRACTICE
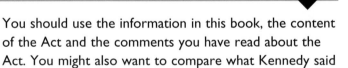

Answer this question as an 8 mark essay

Do you agree that the Civil Rights Act of 1964 made Black Americans 'Free at last'? *Outcome 1*

The question is asking what you know about the Civil Rights Act of 1964.

It also wants you to say if you agree that the Civil Rights Act made Black Americans 'Free at Last'.

You should use the information in this book, the content of the Act and the comments you have read about the Act. You might also want to compare what Kennedy said he wanted to do in his speech on June 11, 1963 with what was really in the Act.

For more advice about layout refer to advice about the 8 mark essays near the end of this book.

18

SELMA, ALABAMA AND THE RIGHT TO VOTE

In this chapter you will find out:
◆ what is meant by voter registration
◆ why it was not easy for Black people to vote
◆ what happened at Selma, Alabama in 1965
◆ why the Voting Rights Act of 1965 was so important.

By 1964 Martin Luther King had became world famous but he knew his work was not finished. Martin Luther King believed that the right to vote without fear or difficulty was vital if Civil Rights was to mean anything at all. As Martin Luther King said in March 1965:

SOURCE 18.1

The Civil Rights Act of 1964 gave Negroes some part of their rightful dignity, but without the vote it was dignity without strength.

THE PROBLEM OF VOTING

Black Americans had been given the right to vote in 1870, but in the years that followed the White people who ran the voter registration offices made it almost impossible for Black Americans to register. In the USA any adult who wants to vote must first of all register to vote.

In many areas of the South, rules made it hard for Black Americans to qualify for the vote. Spelling one word incorrectly on a long registration form or not answering a question correctly could stop a Black person from voting. Martin Luther King summed up the contrast between Black and White Americans who tried to register to vote:

SOURCE 18.2

'Have you ever been asked 100 questions on government just to be able to vote?'

For White supporters of segregation the consequences of allowing Black Americans to vote would be huge. It would end White power in the South. Black politicians would be elected! Martin Luther King's plan to get the vote for Black Americans was to get maximum publicity for the Black citizens who had no voice. The place he chose to launch his campaign was Selma, Alabama.

WHY DID A PROTEST MARCH START IN SELMA, ALABAMA?

Selma, Alabama had 15 000 Black adults who should have had the right to vote, but only 335 had been able to register. In 1963, Civil Rights campaigners began an effort to register Black voters in Dallas County, Alabama. During 1963 and 1964, hundreds of Black Americans who should have had the right to vote freely were prevented from voting by difficulties created when they tried to register at the courthouse in Selma.

In January and February 1965, protests were held in Selma to bring attention to the actions of the White racists who were denying Black Americans their legal rights.

The protests were met by police violence. On February 17, a small Civil Rights march ended in the shooting of Jimmy Lee Jackson who died several days later.

Civil Rights leaders, including Martin Luther King, decided to hold a protest march from Selma to Montgomery on March 7, 1965.

A RISKY PLAN

It was a risky plan which would probably lead to injuries among the demonstrators, but historians now think that was what King and other Black leaders wanted. The Governor of Alabama, George Wallace, had already promised 'Segregation forever!'. The Civil Rights campaign leaders knew very well that a large march from Selma to Montgomery would be met by violent White resistance.

Publicity had worked in Birmingham Alabama, so why should it not work in Selma, Alabama?

KING ARRESTED!

On February 1, 1965, over a month before the march was due to take place, Martin Luther King got himself arrested quite deliberately. After all, he had just gained world wide fame as a Nobel Peace Prize winner so news of his arrest would be big news. It is now clear that this was a sort of publicity stunt. Before he was arrested King and others in the SCLC had prepared a speech that would be sent to newspapers when King was in jail.

SOURCE 18.3 *Even when in jail, Martin Luther King campaigned for civil rights*

On February 5 the New York Times printed the speech.

SOURCE 18.4

Why are we in jail? When the Civil Rights Act of 1964 was passed many decent Americans thought ... the day of difficult struggle was over. By jailing hundreds of Negroes the city of Selma, Alabama has revealed the persisting ugliness of segregation. There are more Negroes in jail with me than there are on the voting registers. This is the USA in 1965. We are in jail because we cannot tolerate these conditions for our nation.

THE MARCH BEGINS

SOURCE 18.5 *King marching in Selma*

Sunday, March 7, 1965 was the starting date for the Selma to Birmingham march.

Approximately 600 marchers started out on the march. When the marchers crossed a bridge on the outskirts of Selma, they were met by about 200 state troopers, and local police mounted on horseback. They were all armed with tear gas, sticks and bull whips. The marchers were ordered to turn back. When they did not, they were attacked by the law enforcement officers. The air filled with tear gas and marchers were beaten, whipped and trampled by the horses. Finally, they turned around and returned to Selma. 17 marchers were hospitalised.

THE USA IS SHOCKED

Television coverage of the march and the attack caused national anger. Sunday, March 7, 1965, 'Bloody Sunday', as the day became known, was a turning point in the campaign for fair voting. All across America people were horrified at what they saw on television and wanted to do something to help the Civil Rights Cause.

George B. Leonard, a journalist who watched the events of 'Bloody Sunday' on TV described his own reaction:

SOURCE 18.6

The chief function (purpose) of the Civil Rights movement has been to awaken the nation's conscience. Hundreds of people dropped whatever they were doing, some would leave home without changing clothes, would borrow money, hitch-hike, board planes, buses and trains, travel thousands of miles with no luggage; all these people would move for a single purpose: to place themselves alongside the Negroes they had watched on television.

THE US ARMY PROTECTS THE MARCH

Dr. King and his supporters went to court and won legal permission to march from Selma to Birmingham. On March 21, the march began again. This time US troops protected the marchers. At the end of the Selma to Birmingham march on March 25, 1965 Martin Luther King spoke to the 25 000 other marchers and once again made it clear what the purpose of the Civil Rights campaign was:

SOURCE 18.7

America's conscience has been sleeping but now it is waking up.
Let us march on segregated housing …
Let us march on segregated schools …
Let us march on poverty …
Let us march on ballot boxes …
Let us march on to the American Dream.

However, within hours of Martin Luther King's speech , four Ku Klux Klan members shot and killed Viola Liuzzo, a White 39-year-old Civil Rights volunteer from Detroit, Michigan. She had travelled south to support the Alabama marchers. President Johnson recognised that prejudice and persecution had ruled too much of the South for too long when he said:

SOURCE 18.8

'Mrs. Liuzzo went to Alabama to serve the struggle for justice. She was murdered by the enemies of justice who for decades have used the rope and the gun to terrorise their neighbours.'

The problem was that violence and intimidation continued.

WAS THE SELMA TO MONTGOMERY MARCH A SUCCESS?

Many people believe that Martin Luther King and the other march planners not only expected violence from White authorities but they even wanted it. The demonstrators knew that TV news would turn public opinion against the White racists and they hoped that televised racist violence would persuade the government to do something about voter registration.

The demonstration in Selma seemed to work! In August, 1965, Congress passed the Voting Rights Act which removed various barriers to registration such as the ability to read and write – which had often been used to stop Black Americans voting.

The 1965 Act was a big move towards making voting rights a reality for thousands of Black Americans in the South. The Act said there were to be no more literacy tests or checks on poll tax payments which had been used to prevent Black Americans from voting.

SOURCE 18.9 *After 1965 many more Black Americans were registered to vote*

HOW SUCCESSFUL WAS THE VOTING RIGHTS ACT?

According to a Federal government report from 1982, it looked like the Act was successful.

- In Mississippi in 1960 there were 22 000 Black Americans registered to vote.
- In Mississippi in 1966 there were 175 000 Black Americans registered to vote.

- In Alabama in 1960 there were 66 000 Black Americans registered to vote.
- In Alabama in 1966 there were 250 000 Black Americans registered to vote.

- In South Carolina in 1960 there were 58 000 Black Americans registered to vote.
- In South Carolina in 1966 there were 191 000 Black Americans registered to vote.

President Johnson publicly advertised the fact that he would sign the new law in the same room where, a century before, President Lincoln signed a document to free slaves who had been made to fight for the Southern Armies in the American Civil War.

Within three years of the Act being passed most of the Black population of the South were registered to vote. That fact also helped improve the living and working conditions of many Black Americans since White politicians now realised they needed Black voters if they wanted to stay in power. Also, many Black Americans now saw an opportunity to become politicians themselves.

The Voting Rights Act marked the end of the Civil Rights campaigns in the south. By 1965 the focus of Civil Rights protests moved north and the style of protest also changed. Non-violence was about to become violent protest.

Chapter Summary
- The last big Civil Rights issue in the South was the right to vote freely.
- White authorities in the South made it difficult for Black Americans to vote easily.
- Martin Luther King led a march to publicise the problems of voting.
- The march was to go from Selma to Birmingham, Alabama.
- Scenes of police attacking the marchers shocked TV viewers across the USA.
- The US government passed the Voting Rights Act in 1965.
- The new act made it much easier for Black Americans to vote.

QUESTION PRACTICE

SOURCE A is adapted from a newspaper report written by George B. Leonard in March 1965.

There are moments when a nation is outraged and that outrage turns to action. One of these moments came when national television showed a group of Negroes at Selma who were gassed, clubbed and trampled by horses.

1 How useful is this source in explaining why support for the Civil Rights campaign increased?   *Outcome 3*

SOURCE B shows the percentage of Black Americans who were registered to vote in four Southern states in 1964 and 1968.

State	1964	1968
Alabama	14	56
Florida	26	62
Georgia	22	56
Mississippi	4	59

2 How did the Voting Rights Act of 1965 help Black Americans? Use Source B and text to answer this question.   *Outcome 1*

QUESTION PRACTICE

3 Explain the importance of the Selma to Birmingham march to the cause of Civil Rights.   *Outcome 2*

19 MALCOLM X AND THE NATION OF ISLAM

In this chapter you will find out:
- why the Civil Rights campaign split in the 1960s
- what the Nation of Islam was
- who Malcolm X was
- how Malcolm X was different from Martin Luther King.

WHY DID THE CIVIL RIGHTS MOVEMENT SPLIT IN THE 1960s?

From the mid 1960s onwards, disagreements increased about what the Civil Rights Movement should do next. There were several reasons for these disagreements:
- Even Martin Luther King had started to wonder if the cost in injuries and human life was worth the gains achieved through non-violent protest.
- The main goals of the campaign had been met. The campaign in the South to end segregation and discrimination was more or less over.
- The problems of Black Americans in the main cities of the North had hardly been touched by the Civil Rights movement in the South.
- Should Civil Rights protests reject non-violence and become more violent?

THE CIVIL RIGHTS MOVEMENT SPLITS

By the mid 1960s the Civil Rights movement had split into two main groups. One part of the movement still supported non-violent protest but the other was prepared to be much more aggressive.

While Martin Luther King had concentrated on Civil Rights issues in the southern states, new ideas and new leaders were growing in the northern cities. Black Americans said that White police officers behaved like bullies in the cities. They were becoming tired of the slow speed of the Civil Rights movement. They were becoming angry with the TV pictures of dogs and water cannons and cattle prods being used on their Black brothers and sisters.

From 1964–1968, many Black leaders rejected integration in favour of Black separatism. They also rejected non-violent protest in favour of self-defense and even aggression. There was a definite split in the Civil Rights movement.

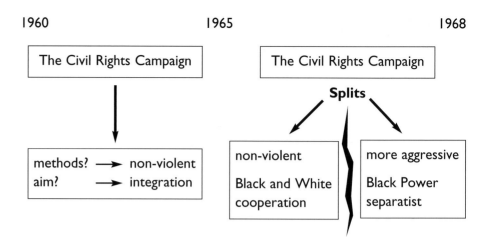

MALCOLM X AND THE NATION OF ISLAM

One of the new leaders was Malcolm X.

FACTFILE

Black Muslims

Black Muslims are members of a religious movement in the United States called the Nation of Islam.

The Nation of Islam was founded in Detroit in 1930.

From 1930 to 1975, the Nation of Islam accepted only Black Americans as members. They considered Whites to be 'devils' and supported the separation of Black Americans and Whites.

In 1934, Elijah Muhammad became the Nation of Islam's leader. He taught three main ideas:
1 The need for Black Americans to establish a separate nation in the United States.
2 The need to have pride in their Black and Muslim identity.
3 The need to run business, shops and services for themselves.
In the 1950s and early 1960s, Malcolm X was the most important spokesman for the Nation of Islam.

One of the groups which rejected the ideas of Martin Luther King was a Black religious group called The Nation of Islam. The Nation of Islam was also called the Black Muslims and it was led by Elijah Muhammad. Malcolm X was the Nation of Islam's most effective speaker and he rejected *integration* in favour of Black *separatism*.

Just as Martin Luther King seemed to represent the spirit of the Southern Black American, Malcolm X came to represent hope for a better future in the Northern ghettos of Chicago, Detroit, and Los Angeles.

WHO WAS MALCOLM X?

Malcolm X was a very different Black leader compared to Martin Luther King. He was born Malcolm Little and his father had been a follower of Marcus Garvey. When Malcolm was a boy, his father was murdered. Some people say the murderers were members of the Ku Klux Klan. Malcolm dropped out of school and moved to Detroit. He became a small time criminal. In prison Malcolm heard of the Nation of Islam for the first time and he liked what he heard.

According to the Nation of Islam the White man is the devil and only Black Americans can cure the ills that afflict them. The Nation of Islam completely rejected the integration ideas of people such as Martin Luther King. Malcolm became a member of the Black Muslims and started to call himself Malcolm X.

Malcolm said that the 'X' in his name represented his real African name which had been stolen by the slave owners who bought and

SOURCE 19.1 *Malcolm X*

sold his ancestors. He refused to use a name that he called his 'slave name'.

HOW DID THE IDEAS OF MALCOLM X DIFFER FROM THOSE OF MARTIN LUTHER KING?

Clearly Malcolm X did not agree with the aims and methods of Martin Luther King.

Malcolm X criticised Martin Luther King's non-violent appeals to 'turn the other cheek' and believed that Black Americans:

SOURCE 19.2

… should stand on our own feet and solve our problems ourselves instead of depending on White people to solve them for us … non-violence is another word for defenceless.

Malcolm X also said:

SOURCE 19.3

The goal of Dr. King is to give Negroes a chance to sit in a segregated restaurant beside the same White folks who have persecuted, beaten and lynched Black people for years. Dr. King seems to want Black people to forgive the people who have beaten, bought, sold, and lynched our people for four hundred years.

MALCOLM X – A THREAT TO THE USA?

Malcolm X was seen as a threat by the Federal government. He was followed everywhere by the *FBI* . His conversations were recorded and his phones were bugged. The US government was afraid that Malcolm X was building up hatred against Whites that could erupt in national riots and revolution. Already there had been riots in Los Angeles. White authority was afraid that they would spread as more and more Black Americans were attracted to the Black Muslims. From Detroit to Selma, from Los Angeles to Mecca in the Middle East, Malcolm's shadow was the FBI.

WHAT DO YOU THINK?

Do you think Malcolm X was a threat?

MALCOLM X LEAVES THE BLACK MUSLIMS

Malcolm X became a very powerful preacher. His message of self help attracted many listeners who were tired of having to wait on White authority to improve conditions. Malcolm X also spoke of a separate nation for Black Americans only.

However as early as 1963, Malcolm X split with the Nation of Islam. Malcolm had serious arguments with the Elijah Muhammad. Malcolm was warned by other followers that there was a plot to kill him. Because of his criticism of Elijah Muhammad, Malcolm X was suspended from the Black Muslims in 1963.

MALCOLM X CHANGES HIS IDEAS

Malcolm X left the Nation of Islam and travelled to Africa and the Middle East.

In the Spring of 1964 Malcolm changed his views after travelling to Mecca. Mecca is one of the holiest places in the Muslim religion. While he was in Mecca, Malcolm X discovered to his surprise that many of his fellow Muslims were also White. Malcolm's experiences in Mecca changed his attitudes to White people. When he returned to the USA he said . . .

SOURCE 19.4

In a few weeks in Africa I saw all races, all colours, blue-eyed blondes to Black-skinned Africans in true brotherhood . . . I now know that some Whites are truly sincere and are capable of being brotherly towards a Black man.

Malcolm X had also changed his views about his former leader Elijah Muhammad. Malcolm called him a 'racist' and a 'faker'.

MALCOLM X IS ASSASSINATED

On February 14, several of Muhammad's followers firebombed Malcolm's home. A week later, on February 21, 1965, Malcolm X was murdered in mysterious circumstances. His bodyguards who were usually with him day and night were 'absent' when three members of the Nation of Islam attacked and killed him.

Chapter summary
- By the mid 1960s the Civil Rights Movement was split between those who wanted to keep using non-violent methods and those who wanted to use more violent methods.
- One group which wanted to use more violent methods was the Nation of Islam.
- The Nation of Islam was known as the Black Muslims.
- The main speaker of the Black Muslims was Malcolm X.
- Malcolm X and the Nation of Islam wanted a separate Black nation for Black Americans.
- Malcolm X and the Nation of Islam did not support integration.
- Malcolm X left the Nation of Islam and was later assassinated by members of 'the Nation'.

QUESTION PRACTICE

SOURCE A is from an interview with Malcolm X in 1964

Dr. King seems to want Black people to forgive the people who have beaten, bought, sold, and lynched our people for four hundred years.

I Explain why Malcolm X thought of White people as his enemy.

Outcome 2

SOURCE B is from a speech by Malcolm X in 1964.

We support your efforts to register our people in Mississippi to vote … But we do not go along with anyone telling us to help non violently. You get your freedom by letting your enemy know that you'll do anything to get your freedom: then you'll get it. It's the only way you'll get it.

2 Describe the ways in which Malcolm X thought Black Americans could win Civil Rights.

Outcome 1

QUESTION PRACTICE

SOURCE C is from a speech by Malcolm X in 1963

Revolution is bloody. Whoever heard of a revolution where they sit around singing 'We shall overcome'? A revolutionary wants his own nation – a Black nation.

SOURCE D is from an interview with Martin Luther King in March 1968.

Most Negroes do not believe in Black separatism. It is very unrealistic and does not help the real problems of today. The real goal is a truly integrated society where there is shared power.

There can be no separate path to power, short of social disaster, that does not recognise the necessity of sharing power with Black hopes for freedom and justice.

3 In what ways did the views of Malcolm X and Martin Luther King differ?

Outcome 3

20 STOKELY CARMICHAEL AND BLACK POWER

In this chapter you will find out:
- why Stokely Carmichael is important to the story of Civil Rights
- what was meant by the slogan 'Black Power'
- in what sense Stokely Carmichael carried on earlier Black Civil Rights ideas.

By the mid 1960s many Black Civil Rights workers were frustrated and impatient with the slow progress being made through non-violent protests. Malcolm X and the Nation of Islam had attracted a lot of support. However it was another leader called Stokely Carmichael who first used the phrase ' *Black Power* ' in 1966.

SOURCE 20.1

SOURCE 20.2 *Stokely Carmichael is remembered as the person who first used the slogan 'Black Power'*

In June 1966, three weeks before his 25th birthday, Stokely Carmichael was elected national chairman of the SNCC and shortly afterwards raised the cry of 'Black power' as he led a freedom march in Mississippi.

SOURCE 20.3 Stokely Carmichael

The only way we gonna stop them White men from whippin' us is to take over. We been sayin' freedom for six years and we ain't got nothin'. What we gonna start sayin' now is Black power.

Stokely Carmichael is probably the best example to show the split that had happened in the Civil Rights movement in the middle of the 1960s. When Carmichael first used the phrase 'Black Power' he was still the chairman of SNCC which stood for Student Non-Violent Coordinating Committee, but his move away from non-violent protest was typical of many Black Americans in the mid 1960s. Stokely Carmichael also changed the aims and eventually the name of the SNCC.

FACTFILE:

Student Nonviolent Coordinating Committee (SNCC) – Part 2

In 1966 the SNCC had a new leader called Stokely Carmichael.

Stokely Carmichael called for a campaign to achieve Black Power.

In 1969 SNCC changed its name to Student National Coordinating Committee, but the organisation broke up soon after that.

What was 'Black Power'?

'Black Power' became a new slogan and a new idea in the Civil Rights movement. In short, the aims of Black Power were as follows:

- Black Americans should not rely on White people to 'give' Civil Rights. Black Americans should build up their own schools, communities, businesses, even hospitals, without interference from Whites.
- Black Americans should be prepared to defend themselves and fight back, using violence if necessary against White attacks.
- Black Americans should develop a pride in their own separate identity and culture as Black people first, and Americans only second.

In some ways the Black Power movement echoed the separatist ideas of Marcus Garvey earlier in the century.

Who was Stokely Carmichael?

It seemed to many young Black Americans that Stokely Carmichael knew what he was talking about. He had been involved in non-violent protest in the early 1960s so when he said it was time to change tactics many people listened.

In 1961, while still a student, Stokely Carmichael had joined the Freedom Rides. He was arrested repeatedly and in one case served a 49-day sentence at one of the hardest prisons in Mississippi, Parchman Farm. Conditions in the prison were described as 'worse than slavery.'

Why did Stokely Carmichael disagree with non-violent protest?

Stokely Carmichael had joined the Student Nonviolent Coordinating Committee (SNCC) because he disagreed with the tactics and leadership of the Southern Christian Leadership Council and Martin Luther King Jr. Members of 'Snick' (as the SNCC was called) wanted a more aggressive struggle against racial segregation in the South.

By 1963, Stokely Carmichael began to disagree with other members of SNCC and other Civil Rights leaders about non-violent protest. He wanted stronger action against the racist violence used against Black Americans in the South. He also wanted to encourage more Black Americans to use the political process to control their own communities.

Stokely Carmichael believed that Black Americans should control the Civil Rights movement and saw no place for White people in the movement. Carmichael repeatedly called for the expulsion of Whites from SNCC.

STOKELY CARMICHAEL AND VOTER REGISTRATION

In some ways Stokely Carmichael had the same aims as the non-violent section of the Civil Rights movement. For example Stokely Carmichael knew it was vital for Black Americans to be able to vote freely.

In March of 1965, Carmichael went to Lowndes County, Alabama, to persuade Black Americans to register for the vote. He wanted to show that it was possible to get Black Americans involved in the political process. He wanted Black voters to use their vote to change the area they lived in. In a county where only 70 Black Americans had been registered to vote in 1964, Carmichael increased the number to over 2,600. Stokely Carmichael also started an all-Black political party, the Lowndes County Freedom Organisation.

WHY DID SOME PEOPLE CRITICISE STOKELY CARMICHAEL?

Some critics of Stokely Carmichael said that the 'Black Power' slogan was racist and too simple. All it did, said his critics, was to make people angry and violent. Stokely Carmichael answered his critics by saying that 'Black Power' simply meant an aim of getting Black Americans control over their political and economic future. He wanted to start separate Black political parties, Black-owned businesses and independent schools for Black Americans. He said:

SOURCE 20.4

We want control of the communities where we live and we want to stop the exploitation of non-White people around the world.

On the other hand Stokely Carmichael did use very violent language which made many young Black Americans angry and violent. For example Carmichael said:

SOURCE 20.5

I am not going to beg the White man for anything I deserve. I'm going to take it.

In 1968 Stokely Carmichael left the SNCC to join an even more extreme Black group called the Black Panthers. You will find out about them in the next chapter. Stokely Carmichael had played a big part in dividing the Civil Rights movement and when he left the SNCC (which had been a non-violent organisation when he became chairman) his replacement as Chairman was H. Rapp Brown. A supporter of the new, radical SNCC summed up the new hard line by saying:

SOURCE 20.6

The White man won't get off our backs so we intend to knock him off ... If it comes the point that Black people must have guns we will have means and ways to obtain those arms.

TWO SYMBOLS OF CHANGE

Two name changes show what happened to the Civil Rights Movement in the 1960s.

The first is the name change of the SNCC. It had been the Student Nonviolent Coordinating Committee but by the end of the 1960s it was called the Student National Coordinating Committee. The word 'nonviolent' had been dropped.

The other name to change was Stokely Carmichael's. By the end of the 1960s he had adopted an African name – Kwame Ture – which showed his rejection of White America and his support for *Black separatism* .

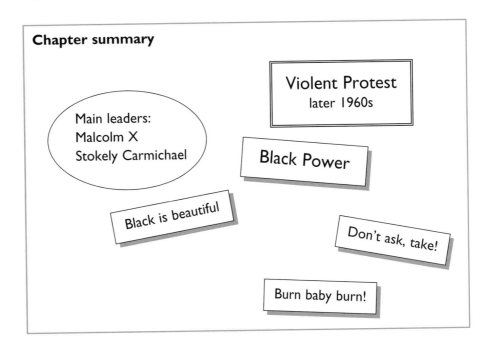

Chapter summary

Main leaders:
Malcolm X
Stokely Carmichael

Violent Protest
later 1960s

Black Power

Black is beautiful

Don't ask, take!

Burn baby burn!

QUESTION PRACTICE

SOURCE A was written by a protest marcher in 1966.

During a protest march in Mississippi we first heard the phrase 'Black Power'. It was immediately supported by young Black Americans who were tired of waiting on changes in the law. They wanted a better life now.

1 Why did young Black Americans support the slogan 'Black Power'?

Outcome 2

SOURCE B is from a diary kept by a White member of the SNCC.

Black power became a cry heard all across America. It inspired young Black Americans to respect themselves and believe in the power of Black people to help themselves without the help of White people. It also inspired fear across White America. They could not separate the ideas of power and violence.

2 What was the effect of the Black Power idea in America?

Outcome 1

QUESTION PRACTICE

The 8 Mark essay

Question:
Why were Stokely Carmichael and Malcolm X important people in the Civil Rights Movement of the 1960s? Outcome 2

THE BLACK PANTHERS

Within a few years in the 1960s the Civil Rights movement had changed. No longer did national TV show pictures of non-violent demonstrators marching down the street singing 'We shall overcome'. New slogans such as 'Burn, baby, burn', 'Black Power' and 'I'm Black and I'm Proud' were heard across the nation.

The media started to focus its attention on the most extreme Black leaders instead of those who believed in non-violence.

By the mid 1960s the USA seemed to be a much more violent place. There were anti-Vietnam war protests going on all across the nation. Riots were breaking out in the cities. President Kennedy had been assassinated. In 1966 a new organisation was started which was called the most violent protest group of the 1960s. It was the Black Panther Party.

FACTFILE

The Black Panthers

The Black Panther Party for Self-Defense was founded in October, 1966, in Oakland, California by Huey P. Newton and Bobby Seale.

The name was shortened to the Black Panther Party. During the mid-1960s, the Black Panthers called for local Black control of services such as education and the police.

The Panthers supported the use of guns – both for self-defense and to retaliate against people who the Panthers said were oppressing the poor. Hostility between the Panthers and the police led to several shoot-outs.

By the mid-1970s the Black Panther Party had ceased to exist.

WHO WERE THE BLACK PANTHERS?

WHY WAS THE NAME BLACK PANTHER CHOSEN?

The name 'Black Panther' was chosen not only because of the word Black but also because the panther is a strong fighter when it is cornered. The leaders of the Black Panthers argued that Black Americans had been cornered by White aggression for a long time and now it was time to defend Black Americans. The Black Panther Party became very popular among young Black Americans who lived in the big cities. By the summer of 1968 a branch of the Black Panthers had been established in most US cities.

DIFFERENT IMAGES OF THE PANTHERS

The Black Panthers represented the complete change that had overtaken the Civil Rights Movement. The image of the early 1960s with Black and White people protesting non-violently was replaced by pictures of Panther members wearing their 'uniform' of black leather jacket, black trousers, black berets and carrying a gun.

SOURCE 21.1 *Most newspapers and TV stations concentrated on the violent and threatening image of the Black Panthers*

SOURCE 21.2 *The Black Panthers started breakfast schemes to help poor children*

SOURCE 21.4 *Huey Newton was the leader of the Black Panthers*

The Panthers supported the use of violence to force change.

When Huey Newton said things like, 'The police have never been our protectors' the big newspapers in the USA and the main TV channels gave the Black Panthers a violent, negative image. Also, since the Panthers had such a violent anti-police and anti-White policy, it is not surprising that city authorities were very suspicious of Black Panther activities.

What was not so well publicised were the self-help programmes launched by the Panthers in their own communities. Panthers not only talked about 'serving the people', they had a policy of doing things to help improve life in the ghettos.

The Black Panthers organised community programmes such as:
◆ free breakfast for children
◆ free health clinics
◆ local school support groups
◆ free clothes for the poor
◆ campaigns for community control of police
◆ campaigns to stop drugs and crime in some of the poorest areas of American cities.

WHAT DID THE BLACK PANTHERS WANT?

The Black Panthers had a ten point programme which included demands for freedom, better housing, better education and the release of all Black people held in prisons.

Panther leaders also spoke about using violence to protect Black communities against White violence. According to Huey Newton their most important demand was:

SOURCE 21.3

… an immediate end to police brutality and murder of Black people.

He also said that Panther patrols should carry guns on the streets of American cities so that they could protect their 'brothers' (other Black people).

SOURCE 21.5

What good was non-violence when the police were determined to rule by force? With guns in our hands we were no longer their subjects but their equals. Out on patrol we stopped whenever we saw the police questioning a brother or sister. We would observe from a safe distance so that the police could not say we were interfering with the performance of their duty. The way we won the brothers (other Black people) over was by patrolling the police with arms.

FBI V THE BLACK PANTHERS

The Panthers were certainly involved in many violent shoot outs across America in the late 1960s.

Police Departments in many cities made regular raids on Panther offices and gun battles sometimes broke out. Many Panthers were arrested.

However recent historians now question how much violence the Panthers caused.

There is evidence to suggest that some of the violence that was blamed on the Panthers was the result of deliberate targeting of the Panthers by police authorities and the US law enforcement agency the FBI.

During the 1960s the FBI spied on many Black leaders. When Black protest groups became more violent the FBI increased its activities to undermine and weaken Black organisations. The FBI called its targets 'Black Nationalist Hate Groups'. Memos sent to FBI agents told them to disrupt the meetings of any Black protest group and especially to prevent the rise of any Black leader who would unify the various protest organisations.

The FBI was also aiming at making Black organisations look bad in order to stop the growth of any White support for the protest groups.

Many of the FBI's actions in the late 1960s were targeted at the Black Panther Party.

The leader of the FBI, J. Edgar Hoover, had said that they should cause as many arguments and divisions within the Black Panther Party as possible. He went on to ask FBI officers to plan ways of destroying the Black Panther Party.

FBI action was also used to destroy the Panther's free breakfast programme to help poor children, hamper the selling of the party's newspaper and to disrupt the Panther's local education classes.

While the FBI said they were protecting law and order many others said the FBI were taking away basic freedoms in America, such as the right to support the political ideas you agree with and the right to print newspapers which may or may not support the government.

HOW IMPORTANT WERE THE BLACK PANTHERS?

Many Black Americans supported the idea of Black Power and the dignity, identity and confidence it gave to Black people. As James Brown the soul singer said, ' Say it loud, we're Black and we're proud!'

However it would be wrong to think that Black Americans were prepared to use violence to improve Civil Rights. Only a small number of them were willing to use the violence that some Black organisations such as the Black Panthers wanted to use. A recent historian summed up the Panthers like this:

SOURCE 21.6

The Panthers were the most violent group to emerge in the late 1960s but by 1969, 27 Panthers were dead and over 700 were in prison. By 1970 the worst was over. The more violent of the Black leaders were either dead or in prison. Many Black Americans realised that all the riots did was to destroy Black property and kill Black people.

The Black Panther Party lost its influence when quarrels among its leaders broke out. By the middle of the 1970s the Black Panther Party no longer existed.

Chapter summary
- The Black Panthers were prepared to use violence.
- The Black Panthers saw the police as the enemy of Black communities.
- The Black Panthers gained publicity because of their threatening image.
- The Black Panthers were also involved in self help schemes in poor cities.
- The Black Panthers supported the anti-White, Black separatist ideas of Stokely Carmichael and Malcolm X.
- The Black Panthers' methods were directly opposite to those proposed by Martin Luther King.

QUESTION PRACTICE

i1

SOURCE A was written by Huey Newton in 1966.

Our ideas are based on the Black Muslims without the religion. I was very impressed with Malcolm X and his ideas on Black separatism. I suppose he meant Black Power, like Stokely said.

1 How useful is this source for finding out about the Black Panther Party? *Outcome 3*

SOURCE B was written by Bobby Seale.

Huey came up with the idea that if you push a panther into a corner, if he can't go left and he can't go right, then he will tend to come out of the corner to wipe out or stop the creature that is attacking it. So I said, 'That's just like Black People. We are just like the Black Panthers.' That's when we decided on our name.

2 Explain why Huey Newton and Bobby Seale chose the name 'Black Panthers'. *Outcome 2*

QUESTION PRACTICE

i2

SOURCE C was written by a special agent for the FBI.

Some of the (Black protest) groups were attempting to change their communities by using violence. When you had the Black Panthers referring to the police as 'Pigs' and spreading a disrespect for law and order I think the government were right to become suspicious of these groups.

SOURCE D is from an interview with Huey Newton.

The first action of the Black Panthers was to go down to a local school with our weapons and be traffic police. Many children had been hit by cars. The police said it would take five years for traffic lights to be put up outside the school.

When the school came out we stopped the traffic. Of course the police came to see why there was a traffic jam. They tried to arrest us for carrying our guns. They were not aware that the law allowed us to carry arms in the street at that time. In three months there was a traffic light in front of the school.

3 Compare sources C and D as evidence of differing views about the Black Panthers. *Outcome 3*

22

THE CIVIL RIGHTS CAMPAIGN MOVES NORTH

In this section you will find out:
- many Black Americans lived in inner city ghettos
- that riots broke out in US cities during the mid 1960s
- Martin Luther King tried to use non-violent methods to improve conditions
- why the Kerner Commission was set up
- what the Kerner Commission said about US society

By the mid 1960s, racial tensions had gone beyond sit ins and freedom rides. The focus of Civil Rights moved to the northern cities.

For Black Americans living in the ghettos of the Northern cities, the issue of desegregation in the South was irrelevant. Their concerns were bad housing, high rents, unemployment, poverty and hunger. Problems of urban gang violence and drug associated crime were also increasing.

Part of the problem facing Martin Luther King was that the public who had watched the Civil Rights campaigns in the South on television thought that Civil Rights had been won after the laws of 1964 and 1965. He knew that big problems still existed in the cities.

SOURCE 22.1

I am appalled that some people feel that the Civil Rights struggle is over because we have a 1964 Civil Rights Act and a Voting Rights Act. Over and over again people ask, what else do you want? Well, let them look around at our big cities.

THE PROBLEMS OF THE GHETTO

Between 1950 and 1960 four million Black Americans had migrated from the South looking for homes and jobs in the northern cities. By 1965 half of all Black Americans lived in the cities of the North. However, many of the Black population lived in run down, slum areas of the cities. These slum areas were known as *ghettos* .

Throughout the twentieth century, Black Americans who migrated to the northern cities found themselves living in poor areas of town where housing was cheapest. Over the years these areas became more and more run down. That was not always the fault of the families that lived there. Often the problem was caused by lack of investment in the area by city authorities. Sometimes the owners of the houses who rented the housing to poor families did not spend money to keep their property up to a high standard.

You will remember that many immigrants from Europe had lived in ghettos when they first arrived in the USA. Usually within a generation those families had saved enough money to move out of the ghettos. However as Black Americans moved into ghetto areas, they found the colour of their skin was an added difficulty in the struggle to escape. The problem of racial discrimination and prejudice was added to the difficulties of breaking out of the 'vicious circle of poverty'.

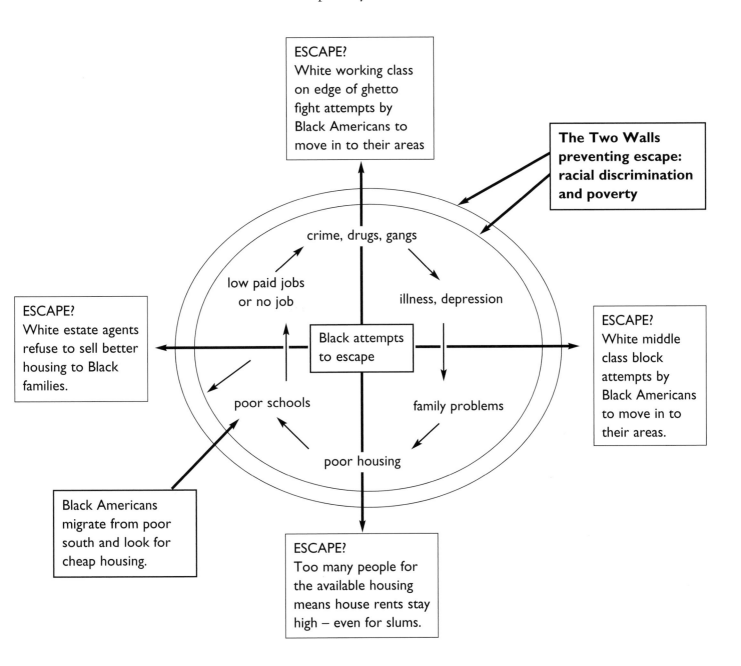

ESCAPE?
White working class on edge of ghetto fight attempts by Black Americans to move in to their areas

The Two Walls preventing escape: racial discrimination and poverty

crime, drugs, gangs

low paid jobs or no job

illness, depression

ESCAPE?
White estate agents refuse to sell better housing to Black families.

Black attempts to escape

ESCAPE?
White middle class block attempts by Black Americans to move in to their areas.

poor schools

family problems

poor housing

Black Americans migrate from poor south and look for cheap housing.

ESCAPE?
Too many people for the available housing means house rents stay high – even for slums.

One teenager summed up the problem of the ghetto when he said:

SOURCE 22.2

In the ghettos the White man has only one handicap. The Black man has two handicaps. He is poor and he is Black.

WATTS, LOS ANGELES

In 1965 the Watts district of Los Angeles erupted into a riot. It was the first of several riots that broke out in many US cities between 1964 and 1967.

In the Watts area of Los Angeles the population was 98% Black but the police force was almost entirely White. To most Black people in the ghetto the police represented White power. The police seemed to be the enemy. The combination of a long hot summer, poverty, unemployment and violent police actions are summed up in the memory of one Watts resident.

SOURCE 22.3

Last night a police officer stopped us and said, 'OK, everybody get off the street!' I said , 'Hey man, it's summer. It's really hot. We don't have air conditioned rooms like you rich White folks. We like to hang out till late in the cool night air. We got no job to get up for in the morning.' But the policeman came at us with his stick and his guns. He beat people on the head. He arrested one guy.

The spark that ignited the riot in Watts was fairly small but was enough to light up tensions that were just below the surface. In August 1965 the police stopped a Black youth for drunk driving. A fight broke out which grew into a confrontation between police and Black residents of Watts. The riot lasted for six days and left 34 dead, 900 wounded and 4000 arrested.

SOURCE 22.4 *Watts 1965 – The first of the urban riots in the 60s*

THE IMPORTANCE OF WATTS

The Watts riot was the first of many city riots that took place across the USA. But it also showed something else. When Martin Luther King went to Los Angeles to try to spread a non-violent message, young Black Americans shouted at him and heckled him. Black Americans in the big cities were not attracted to Martin Luther King's message of non-violence.

The problems of the urban ghettos marked a major turning point in the campaign for Civil Rights. Some historians say that Martin

Luther King lost his focus and the city problems were just too big for him. Others argue that Martin Luther King's message of non-violence was no longer popular and the more violent message of Black Power promised faster results. In some cities such as New York and Philadelphia Black leaders even asked King not to go near them. Chicago, however, invited King to help.

MARTIN LUTHER KING AND CHICAGO

In 1959 the US Commission on Civil Rights had called Chicago, 'the most racially segregated large city in the nation.' The situation had got no better by 1966. In that year Martin Luther King said that Chicago had become the symbol of the race problem in Northern cities. One writer described the problems of Black Americans in Chicago like this:

SOURCE 22.5

Education ... is hardly adequate. There is a Black labour force of 300,000 but few of them have found jobs apart from low paying service jobs such as cleaners or janitors. Negroes make up 23% of the population but they make up 43% of the unemployed.

Black Americans have to pay 10% or 20% more than White Americans to rent or buy a house. Despite that increase in prices, often the quality of houses available to Black Americans was much worse than those available to White house hunters.

THE CHICAGO PLAN

Between 1950 and 1960, 300,000 Black Americans went to Chicago. There were almost one million people in Chicago. Yet the city's Black residents were squeezed into small areas of the city and were unable to find housing outside of those areas. Accusations were made against Mayor Daley of Chicago saying that he organised a system of racial discrimination which kept Black Americans in ghettos and out of White suburbs. It was said that Daley and local estate agents deliberately blocked any Black Americans from moving into 'White' suburbs.

Martin Luther King was keen to get involved in the problems of Chicago because it was an opportunity to see if the non-violent approach used in the South would be successful in the North.

In January 1966 Martin Luther King and the SCLC made a proposal for the development of a non-violent action plan to improve the Chicago area. The proposal was known as the Chicago Plan.

MARCHES AND VIOLENCE

A few months before the Chicago Plan, the SCLC made an alliance with Chicago's community organisations. The new organisation was called the Chicago Freedom Movement. The focus of the new movement was the issue of fair housing.

When the Chicago Freedom Movement began to march into White-only areas of Chicago it was met by mobs of Whites. In July 1966, marchers were attacked with stones and bottles. One march of 350 was met by a mob of 4000. Finally, at the end of August, city leaders met with Dr. King and agreed to a programme of fair housing.

However tensions in Chicago went deeper than the issue of housing. Race tension had erupted in riots in 1919. The same thing happened in 1966.

RIOT!

Chicago got hotter and hotter in the summer of 1966. On July 12 police shut down a fire hydrant that had been opened by Black teenagers wanting to cool down. A fight broke out. Ten people were injured, windows smashed and some shops looted. Mayor Daley dismissed it as unimportant kids' crime. Martin Luther King called it a riot. On the next night sniper fire, petrol bombs and stoning of city firemen seemed to support King's description.

SOURCE 22.6 *Chicago erupted into riots in 1966*

THE RESULTS OF THE CHICAGO RIOTS

◆ The US government passed another Civil Rights Act in 1968. Part of it contained a Fair Housing Act, which banned discrimination in the selling or renting of housing because of race, color, religion or sex.
◆ The Chicago riots also weakened Martin Luther King's influence. Many people were more attracted to calls for 'Black Power'. If Martin Luther King couldn't prevent riots and make a real difference to life in the ghetto then perhaps he was irrelevant to the needs of Black Americans in the late 1960s. The SNCC issued a poster in Chicago saying 'Wake up brothers – who speaks for you?'. It was an obvious attack on Martin Luther King.

SOURCE 22.8 *Riots spread to many US cities. This picture shows a block of Detroit in flames.*

As Linda Bryant, a previous supporter of King said:

SOURCE 22.7

By the summer of 1966 Stokely Carmichael's call for Black Power had reached Chicago. The idea appealed to many Black Americans in Chicago. When Dr King decided that Black Power was going to be something that we should hush a little bit, I think that made it even more attractive to us.

More riots followed during the long hot summers of the next few years. In 1966 there were another 43 'race riots' but despite extra government money for schools, housing, jobs and health programmes the looting, rioting and killing continued. Civil Rights leaders condemned the violence but young Black Americans refused to listen. One of the most destructive riots was in Detroit. Several people were killed and millions of dollars worth of property was destroyed. After the Detroit riot President Johnson ordered an official investigation into the causes of the urban riots. The investigation was called the Kerner Commission after the man in charge, Otto Kerner.

THE KERNER COMMISSION

When the Kerner Commission made its report the USA was shocked by what it said.

> **What the Kerner Commission discovered:**
> - The USA was divided into two societies – one Black and poor, the other White and richer
> - 40% of all Black Americans lived in poverty
> - Black men were twice as likely to be unemployed as White men
> - Black men were three times as likely to be in low skilled jobs as White men
> - The riots and other crimes were caused by poverty

The final report of the Kerner Commission said that the riots were caused by a White society that did not seem to care about Black Americans.

The conclusion of the report said that White society created the ghettos, White society kept them going and White society did nothing to improve them.

WHAT HAPPENED BECAUSE OF THE KERNER COMMISSION?

The President did little about most of the Kerner Commission's report. Few of the report's recommendations were accepted or put into operation.

The riots had turned White Americans, and even middle class Black Americans, against the cause of Civil Rights. There were few votes to be gained by supporting Civil Rights.

However, a new Civil Rights Act was passed in 1968. It was the last important Civil Rights law of the 1960s.

The first point was positive and helpful. It seemed to accept the complaints made by Martin Luther King about housing in Chicago and other cities.

However the second point was negative. It aimed at stopping the spread of riots. If Black leaders who supported violent protest moved from one state to another they could be arrested on suspicion of spreading plans about riots.

> **The Civil Rights Act of 1968:**
>
> 1 Banned discrimination in the sale or rental of housing.
> 2 Made it a federal crime to move from one state to another to help cause a riot.

It showed that President Johnson was aware that many White voters were losing patience with the violent tactics of Civil Rights protesters.

Chapter summary
- Conditions in the Black ghettos of the northern cities were very bad.
- Riots erupted in the cities in the mid 1960s.
- Martin Luther King tried to use non-violent methods to improve life in the northern cities.
- Martin Luther King was only partly successful.
- New ideas about Black Power were more attractive.

QUESTION PRACTICE

SOURCE A is from an interview with Ed Vaughan who took part in the Detroit riots in 1967.

It wasn't Black Power that caused the rebellion, it was the lack of power. People did not see any hope. People were beginning to be unemployed more and more. We were stuck in the ghetto.

1 Why is Source A useful for finding out about the Detroit riots in 1967?

Outcome 3

SOURCE B is from a TV interview with Nathan Hampton, a Black American who lived in a US city ghetto.

We were trapped in the ghetto. We had low pay jobs so that meant poor houses. We had bad schools so that meant we got no education. We had drugs gangs messin' up our kids. By fighting back we felt that we had finally gotten the White community to listen to some of the concerns that we had been talking about for years.

2 What were the causes of the US city riots in the 1960s?

Outcome 1

QUESTION PRACTICE

SOURCE C is from an interview with Martin Luther King on March 25, 1968.

If the problem isn't dealt with we will continue to move, as the Kerner Commission said, towards two societies, one White, one Black, separate and unequal. The problems facing us are bad housing and poor education and improper health facilities.

SOURCE D was said by Ron Scott who was a 20 year old factory worker living in Detroit.

A lot of people felt it couldn't happen in Detroit, because people had good jobs, they had homes and generally it was a good time. But you can't always judge things by how they appear on the surface. Inside of most Black people there was a time bomb. There was a pot that was about to overflow, and there was rage that was about to come out. The riot provided an opportunity for that to happen.

3 To what extent do Sources C and D agree about the causes of the urban riots of the 1960s?

Outcome 3

23

THE ASSASSINATION OF MARTIN LUTHER KING

In this chapter you will find out:
- by 1968 Martin Luther King was losing a lot of support
- by 1968 Martin Luther King had made many enemies
- in 1968 Martin Luther King tried once again to use non-violent protest
- in 1968 Martin Luther King was assassinated.

After more than ten years leading the Civil Rights movement Martin Luther King had to adjust to a changing world.

He was certainly becoming less optimistic about change through non-violence.

He was becoming less popular with young Black Americans.

He was upset by the US government's failure to spend enough money to help the poor of America.

MARTIN LUTHER KING HAD MADE HIMSELF SOME ENEMIES

- *King attacked the Vietnam War.*
  When Martin Luther King criticised US involvement in the expensive Vietnam War he lost the support of the US government. He said the US government was spending a fortune on death and destruction and not nearly enough on making life better for the poor of America.

  A supporter of King summed up his point:

SOURCE 23.1

Although Black people made up only 10% of the population of the USA our brothers make up 40% of the ordinary soldiers fighting in the jungles of Vietnam. We've got to ask 'Why'? Is the war just a neat way to get Black youth out of the country? If we are good enough to fight for freedom in the name of the USA why can't we be free in our own country?

- *The FBI saw King as a possible threat to the safety of the USA.*
  Over the years, the FBI did everything it could to undermine the Civil Rights movement and discredit Martin Luther King. The FBI even paid some Black Americans to stir up trouble and try to cause riots at non-violent demonstrations. Later, FBI files showed that they had also planned times when they could have assassinated King if they had wanted to.
- *The challenge of Black Power.*
  The Nation of Islam and the Black Panthers were rapidly increasing their numbers in many cities around the country. Their speeches constantly attacked the ideas of Martin Luther King, especially non-violence and integration.

DID MARTIN LUTHER KING CHANGE HIS IDEAS?

Despite increasing pressure to change his ideas to attract new support Martin Luther King stuck to what he believed in.

◆ Martin Luther King still disagreed with the separation ideas of Black Muslims. To explain his point he said:

SOURCE 23.2

The American Negro is neither totally African nor totally western. He is Afro-American ... a combination of two cultures ... The solution to our problem will not come through seeking to build a separate nation within a nation ... America must be a nation in which its people are partners in power.

◆ Martin Luther King still believed that the support of White people was vital if more Civil Rights were to be won. As he said:

SOURCE 23.3

In the years to come Negroes will continue to need the support they had in the years past. Ten percent of the country (Black Americans) cannot by anger and violence alone induce (cause) ninety percent of the country to change its way of life.

Martin Luther King intended to show America that he could still use non-violent protest to improve people's lives. Some people believe that by the middle of the 1960s he was trying to do too much. Instead of Black Civil Rights Martin Luther King seemed to be campaigning for widespread Human Rights by attacking city problems, poverty and what he believed to be an unfair war being fought by the USA against North Vietnam.

KING GOES TO MEMPHIS

In 1968 Martin Luther King was planning another march on Washington. It was to be a Poor People's March to protest about poverty in the cities.

However, two weeks before the march, King went to Memphis, Tennessee to support a strike by rubbish collectors. Most of them were Black and very poorly paid.

A peaceful march in support of the strikers turned out to be anything but peaceful. A full scale riot broke out and King was very embarrassed. Two weeks later, he returned to Memphis. He was determined to lead a peaceful march in the city.

SOURCE 23.4 *Martin Luther King (second from right) took time out from his Chicago plan to go south to Memphis*

'I'VE SEEN THE PROMISED LAND'

The night before the planned march, he made his last speech. It became famous because it seemed as if Martin Luther King was aware that he would die soon.

SOURCE 23.5

We've got some difficult days ahead. ... Like anybody I would like to live a long life ... but I'm not concerned about that now ... I've seen the promised land. I may not get there with you but I want you to know that we as a people will get to the promised land.

KING SHOT DEAD

After the speech King stood on the balcony of his motel room.

SOURCE 23.6 *This photograph was taken seconds after Martin Luther King was shot. These people are pointing to where the shot came from.*

As he stood there, an escaped convict called James Earl Ray shot and killed Martin Luther King. The date was April 4, 1968. Martin Luther King was only 39 years old.

He had been worried about his safety. Martin Luther King had received many death threats which he took seriously. President John F. Kennedy had been assassinated. Medger Evers, a well known Civil Rights worker had been murdered. Malcolm X had been killed. However, Martin Luther King knew that if he was to achieve any more improvements in the lives of Americans he had to keep grabbing headlines.

The headlines on April 5 were not what he had intended.

When word spread of Martin Luther King's death, riots erupted in 168 cities. 70 000 US troops were needed to restore order.

It seemed that the non-violent Civil Rights movement had finally died with Martin Luther King.

SOURCE 23.7 *The world was shocked by the assassination of Martin Luther King. These headlines are from British newspapers*

WAS MARTIN LUTHER KING IMPORTANT?

For many people Martin Luther King was the man who represented the Civil Rights Movement. He forced changes so that life in America, especially in the South, was very different in 1965 to what it had been in 1955.

In the 1980s the Black mayor of Atlanta, Georgia (a state in the South) said that as a boy growing up he was scared of doing anything to offend a White person. Now he was the mayor – thanks to changes caused by Martin Luther King.

Even Stokely Carmichael said that Martin Luther King was the one man the masses of Black Americans would listen to.

However not all people thought that Martin Luther King was a good man. A White steel worker said:

SOURCE 23.8

If a bunch of Ku Kluxers had got hold of Martin Luther King, he wouldn't have lived as long as he did.

Perhaps the effect of Martin Luther King is best summed up by his friend Jesse Haley, who said:

SOURCE 23.9

He gave people a dream to live for.

Chapter summary
- By 1968 Martin Luther King had made many enemies and had lost a lot of support.
- Most young Black Americans were more attracted to Black Power ideas.
- Martin Luther King tried to use non-violent methods to attack the problems of poverty and unemployment.
- When he went to Memphis to lead a protest, Martin Luther King was shot dead.
- Nearly every Black American and most Whites agree that Martin Luther King was one of the most important leaders of any colour in the twentieth century.

QUESTION PRACTICE

SOURCE A is from an article comparing life in the USA in 1960 to life in 1980

In 1960 most places in the South were still segregated.
In 1960 most Black Americans did not vote.
By 1983 there were Black mayors in 240 towns and cities.
By 1980 nearly all the schools in the south were integrated and there was a big increase in the numbers of Black students at college.

1 Describe the ways in which race relations in the USA improved between 1960 and 1980. *Outcome 1*

SOURCE B is from a recent book about America in the 1960s.

In 1968 George Wallace, who had been the governor of Alabama during the Birmingham demonstrations, tried to become US President. He got 10 million votes in the 1968 election. He promised to bring back segregation.

2 How useful is source B as information about how far the Civil Rights campaigns had changed life in America? *Outcome 3*

QUESTION PRACTICE

Answer this question as an 8 mark essay:

How important was Martin Luther King? *Outcome 1*

CONCLUSION
FREE AT LAST?

In 1968 the Olympic Games were held in Mexico City. When two Black American athletes won silver and gold medals in a race they mounted the winners' platform. America was shocked and embarrassed by what happened next.

As the American flag was raised and the National Anthem was played, the two athletes, called John Carlos and Tommie Smith, dropped their heads, refused to look at the flag and raised their right hands in a Black Power salute. On their right hands they wore black gloves. It was a message that some Black Americans did not feel they belonged to the USA and that the athletes were supporters of Black Power.

In 1968 it seemed that America was still divided over race.

Since then Black TV and film stars have become internationally popular. Black music which was once banned from White TV and radio stations is now popular everywhere. There are many more Black Americans in powerful jobs. Nobody seems to bother about skin colour any more. Or do they?

Are Black Americans really Free at Last? Is America a fully integrated society?

Think about the next two pieces of information.

In the 1990s a new Black leader called Louis Farrakhan became more popular.

His ideas are linked directly to Marcus Garvey, the Nation of Islam, Malcolm X and Stokely Carmichael. Louis Farrakhan wants Black Americans to be entirely separate from White Americans. If Louis Farrakhan represents the future it would seem that Black Americans are still unhappy with their lives in the USA.

In June 1998 a Black American called James Byrd was walking home in a small town in Texas called Jasper. He was kidnapped, tortured and murdered by men linked to the Ku Klux Klan. James Byrd was killed because he was Black. It happened more than 30 years after Martin Luther King's 'Dream speech' and the Civil Rights Acts of the 1960s.

So is America the land of the free? Are Black Americans free at last? Or did an American president get it right when he said that laws can change what people do but nothing can change how people feel or what people think? What do you think?

SOURCE 24.1 *The Mexico Olympics were used for Black Power protest and publicity*

HOW TO WRITE YOUR 8 MARK ESSAY

One of the questions in internal tests and the final exam at Intermediate 2 is the 8 mark essay question. It is an explanation type of question for which you usually have to explain the reasons for or results of something.

REMEMBER THAT YOUR ESSAY

- must have an introduction
- must have a middle section with paragraphs for each of your main points
- must have a separate conclusion.

Making a Plan

It often helps to jot down a list of about five main points you want to deal with before you start your essay. You can add to the list if more points occur to you.

Introduction

This is worth 1 or 2 marks. It should deal with the question. It might only be a sentence or two. You could start with a sentence like this: *There were many reasons why ... (such and such happened). These reasons were ...*

Middle section. This is worth 5 marks

If you have five main points you should have five paragraphs in the middle section of your essay. Each paragraph should start with a sentence which lays out what the paragraph will be about. You should then explain what your main point means or how it is connected to the question. You then go on to use accurate and relevant facts to explain what you mean and show off what you know.

Conclusion. This is worth 2 marks

It should be a paragraph of a few sentences.
It should sum up your answer. It could be something like this:
In conclusion, there were lots of reasons why ... (such and such happened). These reasons included ... (sum up your main points)
In your conclusion you should:
- Sum up the points you have explained earlier in the answer. You could also say which points you think were the most important and give reasons.
- Make up your mind and answer the question that you were asked.

Use this pattern for all your 8 mark essays. You can also use it to help you with your extended response. Remember you only have to do one 8 mark essay in the exam. Use the advice on this page to help you get it right.

The following example shows how an 8 mark essay can be

structured. The question is: *Why did attitudes towards immigration change in the 1920s?*

Introduction

You could start with a sentence like this: *There were many reasons why attitudes towards immigration changed in the 1920s. These reasons were ...* (use the five phrases from the spider diagram in Chapter 3.)

Main chapter

You should have made five points in your introduction so these points should be developed into five paragraphs – one paragraph for each point. Each paragraph should start with a main sentence which lays out what the paragraph will be about.

Your first paragraph could start like this:
The first reason why attitudes changed towards immigrants in the 1920s is because Americans were afraid that immigrants might take their jobs away.

Now you should use information from the text to explain what you mean.

Your next paragraphs should follow the same pattern. That means your next paragraphs should have a starting sentence that introduces what each paragraph will be about.

Conclusion

Your conclusion should sum up your answer. It could be something like this:
There were lots of reasons why attitudes to immigrants changed in the 1920s. Immigrants were seen as a threat. They were a threat to jobs, to housing, they might bring revolution and they might commit crimes. All these fears existed in the 1920s and help explain why attitudes changed. I think the most important of these reasons were ...

In this conclusion you have:

1 referred to the main question
2 shown that you know there were several reasons for the changing attitudes
3 decided which reasons, in your opinion, were the most important
4 made a direct answer to the main question.

Now try to write your own answer to the main question using the ideas on this page to help you.

Well done.

Refer back to this structure when writing other extended answers. You can use it to deal with all sorts of extended-answer questions.

EXTENDED RESPONSE ADVICE (INTERMEDIATE 2 ONLY)

Intermediate 2 candidates must also produce a longer prepared essay as part of the external course assessment – usually in February/March.

This is called the Extended Response and is worth one quarter of the final marks. It is similar to the 8 mark short essay, but the main differences are:

◆ It will be much longer than an 8 mark short essay. You will have an hour to write it. It could be up to 1000 words long (four or five sides of A4).

◆ You choose your own question relating to one of the three units making up your course. Your teacher can advise you on this.

◆ You research and prepare your answer by reading and taking notes from a variety of sources. Your teacher can help you with sources.

◆ You prepare a plan of 150 words with sub-headings which you can take into the final writing-up session. Your teacher can check your plan for you.

◆ A teacher will supervise the final one-hour writing-up session under exam conditions, but cannot help you in any way. Your plan and response are then sent to the SQA for marking.

Choosing a question

Pick a topic that interests you and that you feel you can do well in. Discuss the exact wording of the question with your teacher.

Choose a question that requires you to explain and assess what happened rather than simply describing events.

Avoid questions which cover too much or which are too vague or too narrow.

You should be able to divide it up into about five sub-headings.

Some possible questions from this unit are given on the next page.

Reading and note-taking

Talk to your teacher about sources.

As you read, jot down notes for your different sub-headings (either using separate sheets for each sub-heading or by indicating in the margin which sub-heading each note is about).

Use key words and avoid copying whole sentences and paragraphs – try to use one or two good short quotes.

Preparing your plan

Use your notes to prepare your 150 word plan.

This should consist of sub-headings and key points to remind you of what you want to include.

You could also draw a spider diagram like the one on the next page to help you.

If you want, you can write a practice draft of your full response, but you cannot take it into the final write-up session with you.

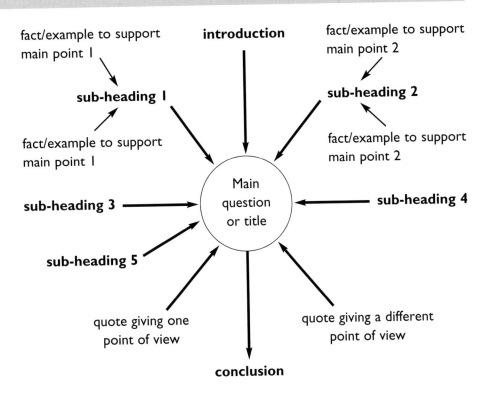

fact/example to support main point 1

sub-heading 1

fact/example to support main point 1

introduction

fact/example to support main point 2

sub-heading 2

fact/example to support main point 2

sub-heading 3

Main question or title

sub-heading 4

sub-heading 5

quote giving one point of view

quote giving a different point of view

conclusion

You are only allowed to take in your plan of **not more than 150 words**.

The write-up session

Your plan will enable you to work your way steadily through your response.

You have one hour to do this, allowing about 10 minutes for each sub-heading and leaving time for your conclusion.

Try to concentrate on explanation and analysis rather than just description and narrative.

If you are running out of time, make quick notes about any remaining sub-heading(s) and go straight to your conclusion.

THE EXTENDED RESPONSE – SOME SUGGESTIONS

In order to do well in your extended response you will need to choose a question that will allow you to show off what you know and also use your information to answer a question rather than just tell a story.

The following titles are only suggestions. You can make up your own questions.

◆ What difficulties did immigrants to the USA face in the early years of the twentieth century?
◆ For what reasons did attitudes to immigrants change by 1930?
◆ Why did the 'Open Door' policy on immigration change?
◆ Why was the Supreme Court decision of 1896 so important to the lives of Black Americans?
◆ To what extent did fear and prejudice affect the lives of Black Americans living in the south before 1954?
◆ How important were the Ku Klux Klan in preventing Black Americans gaining Civil Rights?
◆ To what extent did the trial of the Scottsboro Boys and the Emmett Till case show the world that it was difficult for Black Americans to get fair treatment in Southern law courts?
◆ Is it true to say that Du Bois, Garvey and Washington had the same aims but different methods?
◆ Why was World War Two important to the cause of Civil Rights?
◆ Was the Montgomery Bus Boycott important?
◆ Was the non violent campaign of Martin Luther King successful?
◆ How important to the cause of Civil Rights was Martin Luther King?
◆ Why did the Civil Rights campaign split in the mid 1960s?
◆ Did Black Power do more harm than good to the Civil Rights campaign?
◆ Was Malcolm X important to the Civil Rights campaign?
◆ Why did many Black Americans decide to migrate north?
◆ Were the sit ins and Freedom Rides successful?
◆ Why was the Supreme Court decision of 1954 so important for Civil Rights in the USA?

A NOTE ON SOURCES AND SUPPORT MATERIAL

The two best collections of eye witness accounts/primary sources are *The Eyes on the Prize Civil Rights Reader* published by Penguin in 1991 and *Voices of Freedom* published by Vintage in 1995. Each chapter in both books are put in context by short essays and each source has its own introduction.

The Eyes on the Prize series also has associated videos but customers purchasing over the Internet should be wary of buying US videos which may not be compatible with UK machines.

For pupil use, probably the best source is the Internet where a search put on 'Civil Rights' or 'Afro/American' or any significant character or event will yield many sites ranging from university lectures to pictorial museums and US school sites. Teachers should be wary of searching under Ku Klux Klan.

Reference CD-ROMs are useful, particularly *Grolier* and *Encarta*. Both have good search engines for key words and articles are supported by photos.

The Chronicle series of encyclopaedia type books from Longmans are useful, particularly the *Chronicle of 20th century* (also on CD Rom) and the *Chronicle of America*. However they require the user to have a specific search in mind otherwise the sheer volume of information can be daunting and also very distracting.

Videos are also very useful for illustrating and developing the course and a few of these are listed below.

The Diary of Miss Jane Pitmann (Cecily Tyson) charts the life of a black woman from her birth in the 1850s to her death in the mid 1960s. Her life charts the main issues in Black American History during that time. The film is not easily available in this country but can be found on Internet video listings.

More accessible is the *Roots* series, still available on video. The earlier episodes dealing with slavery and the nineteenth century may be irrelevant but the later episodes in the twentieth century are very good.

Malcolm X (Denzil Washington) is a long (three hours) movie dealing with the politics and events of the 1950s and 60s and could be edited for school use.

Mississippi Burning (Gene Hackman) may not be suitable for all but it does deal with FBI investigations into the Ku Klux Klan and the wider issues of racism in the Deep South.

Programmes made for schools and colleges in the late 1990s include Channel 4's *Heroes and Villains*, a 20 minute film on Martin Luther King, while Part Five of the BBC's series *Black People of Americas* is particularly useful, dealing as it does with the whole Civil Rights movement of the 1950s and 60s.

GLOSSARY

amendment	change to the US constitution
American Dream	the belief that anyone, if they work hard, can be a success in the USA
Black Power	a slogan in the 1960s supported by Black Americans who wanted to fight back
Black separatism	an idea that Black Americans should live separate lives in communities completely separate from Whites
boycott	a way of putting pressure on someone by not using their services
bribery	offering money or favours to influence someone
Civil Rights movement	a campaign by Black Americans for equality with White people
communism	a way of living whereby all land and property is equally owned by everyone
constitution	the rules by which a country is run
desegregate	the opposite of segregation, meaning to allow anyone of any colour access to the same facilities
discrimination	treating people differently, often unfairly
emigration	the movement of people away from their home country
executive order	the right of the President of the USA to make an order without discussion with the US government
FBI	the Federal Bureau of Investigation – a nation-wide law enforcement agency
Federal ...	anything to do with national law in the USA
immigration	the arrival of people in a new country
integration	mixing people of all races together
lynching	the torture and murder of Black Americans suspected of breaking the law
melting pot	the belief that different people from all over the world would mix together in the USA and become 'American'
migrate	the movement of people from one place to another
Nobel Peace Prize	a prize awarded every year to a person or group who has done the most for world peace
open door policy	the idea that anyone from anywhere could go to the USA and settle there
persecution	picking on someone or some group of people
prejudice	prejudging people before knowing them as individuals
quota system	controlling the number of immigrants by setting a maximum number allowed in each year
revolution	the majority getting together and overthrowing the established government
segregation	keeping Black and White people apart
separate but equal	keeping Black and White people apart by providing separate but equal facilities for them
Urban ghetto	part of a city, often a slum, where one particular group of people live
Wasp	White Anglo Saxon Protestant – people who thought they were better than other people

INDEX